Shojo Beat

Kaze Hikaru

28

Story & Art by

Taeko Watanabe

Contents

Story Thus Far

It is the end of the Bakufu era, the second year of Keio (1866). The Shinsengumi is a band of warriors formed to protect the shogun.

Tominaga Sei, the daughter of a former Bakufu *bushi*, joined the Shinsengumi disguised as a boy by the name of Kamiya Seizaburo to avenge her father and brother. She has continued her training under the only person in the Shinsengumi who knows her true identity, Okita Soji, and she aspires to become a true *bushi*.

The Choshu and Satsuma hans sign a secret agreement, and the two regions build up arms as the vanguard of the anti-Bakufu front. Meanwhile, Ito takes Sei hostage in order to lure Hijikata to his territory and propose a secret partnership, but Hijikata rejects him and his plans are foiled. The prickly relationship between Hijikata and Sei eases slightly when they both realize they share an ultimate goal of protecting Captain Kondo.

Characters

Tominaga Sei
She disguises herself as a boy to enter the Mibu-Roshi. She trains under Soji, aspiring to become a true *bushi*. But secretly, she is in love with Soji.

Okita Soji
Assistant vice captain of the Shinsengumi and licensed master of the Ten'nen Rishin-ryu. He supports the troop alongside Kondo and Hijikata and guides Seizaburo with a kind yet firm hand.

Kondo Isami
Captain of the Shinsengumi and fourth grandmaster of the Ten'nen Rishin-ryu. A passionate, warm and well-respected leader.

Hijikata Toshizo
Vice captain of the Shinsengumi. He commands both the group and himself with a rigid strictness. He is also known as the "Oni vice captain."

Saito Hajime
Assistant vice captain. He was a friend of Sei's older brother. Sei is attached to him in place of her lost brother.

Ito Kashitaro
Councilor of the Shinsengumi. A skilled swordsman and an academic with anti-Bakufu sentiments, he plots to sway the direction of the troop.

SECOND YEAR OF KEIO (1866)
SUMMER
KYOTO, NISHI HONGANJI
SHIN-SENGUMI HEAD-QUARTERS
SO...
I WENT DOWN TO THAT OLD TEMPLE RUMORED TO BE HAUNTED BY A BEAUTIFUL GHOST...
...WITH A FRIEND OF MINE.
IT WAS A HOT, STEAMY NIGHT WITH ONLY ONE STAR SHINING DOWN.
KAZE HIKARU SENRYU
THE PATH OF LOVE CUT OPEN BY THE PATH OF ONI
By Mariko-san from Aichi

ONCE WE ENTERED THE TEMPLE, THERE WAS A LOOOONG CORRIDOR, AND...
UH-HUH...
WHAT ARE YOU DOING, HARADA SENSEI?!
A BUSHI SHOULD NOT BE SITTING AROUND HALF-NAKED!
ARE YOU AWARE THAT YOU ARE MEANT TO BE A ROLE MODEL FOR YOUR SUB-ORDINATES?!
DON'T BE SO HARSH. IT'S BOILING HOT OUT.
CON-STANTLY TESTING THE LIMITS OF YOUR ENDUR-ANCE ISN'T SO HEALTHY EITHER, YOU KNOW, KAMIYA?
SO I CAN AT LEAST TELL A TALE THAT WILL GIVE US ALL THE CHILLS. JOIN US!
A GHOST STORY?
THAT'S RIGHT.
SO THEN I HEARD THE SOUND OF WATER, "SPLISH... SPLISH..." COMING FROM THE DARKNESS OF THE CORRIDOR.

AND THEN!
THAT WAS WHEN I NOTICED THAT A SOAKING-WET FIGURE WAS STANDING RIGHT BEHIND ME!!
PLIIP
AAAAAAAAH!!
HA HA HA HA HA!
YOU SHOULD'VE SEEN THE EXPRESSION ON YOUR FACE, KAMIYA-SAN!
O-O-OKITA SENSEI?!
HEY, SOJI. YOU JUMPED IN SOME WATER? THAT MUST HAVE FELT GOOD.
YES.
I WAS OUT MAKING MY ROUNDS AND ENDED UP SO DRENCHED IT WAS LIKE I HAD FALLEN INTO A RIVER, SO I DECIDED I MIGHT AS WELL TAKE A SWIM IN THE HORI RIVER. ♡

HUMPH!! YOU ALWAYS GOOF AROUND LIKE THIS!!
THE FLOOR IS A PUDDLE! HURRY UP AND TAKE YOUR KIMONO OFF!!
WHAT?
UM, WAIT A MIN...
AH.
KAMIYA'S BEING THE HELPFUL WIFE AS ALWAYS. ♡
IT'S NOT LIKE THAT!!
KAMIYA-SA—!!
FWIP
AIYEEE!!
SORRY.
MY LOIN-CLOTH GOT WASHED AWAY IN THE RIVER.
HUH?! HEY, KAMIYA!
YOU NEVER SCREAM WHEN YOU SEE MINE, SO HOW COME YOU'RE SO SHOCKED TO SEE SOJI'S?

I-I'VE GOTTEN USED TO SEEING YOURS!!
YOU SHOW IT TO ME PRACTICALLY EVERY DAY AS A GREETING, HARADA SENSEI!!!
HUH?!
I CAN'T FLIRT WITH OTHER WOMEN...
...SO I FIGURE IT'LL CHEER ME UP A BIT...
...IF CUTE KAMIYA SEEMS SLIGHTLY INTERESTED, EVEN THOUGH HE'S A GUY...
FLIRT?!
YOU WENT TO SO MUCH TROUBLE TO MARRY OMASA-SAN, AND NOW YOU'RE GOING TO BETRAY HER?!
THAT'S WHY I'M NOT GONNA ACTUALLY GO OUT AND FLIRT WITH WOMEN!
BUT YOU CAN'T BLAME ME FOR FEELING A LITTLE LONELY AFTER BEING ALONE FOR SO LONG.
BEING ALONE ...
ARE YOU SAYING OMASA-SAN LEFT YOU?!

NO.
SHE'S HOME, BUT WE SLEEP IN DIFFERENT ROOMS, SO...
Sigh
ARE YOU TWO GETTING BORED WITH YOUR MARRIAGE ?!
ARE YOU SERIOUS ?!
SHE'S GIVING BIRTH TO OUR FIRST CHILD THIS MONTH!!
AAH ...!!
RIGHT! YOU TOLD US ABOUT THAT!
OOOH, I CAN'T WAIT. ♡
AND? HOW IS OMASA-SAN DOING?
HOW IS SHE?
OMASA IS ABSO-LUTELY...
...GREAT!!

THE BREASTS OF A PREGNANT WOMAN ARE IN-CREDIBLE!
THEY LOOK SO NICE THAT YOU FEEL LIKE YOU ABSOLUTELY HAVE TO FONDLE THEM! BUT...
I'M SORRY, SANO-SAN.
IF I LET YOU TOUCH THEM JUST A LITTLE, YOU PROBABLY WON'T BE ABLE TO STOP...
SO PLEASE CONTROL YOURSELF UNTIL THE BABY IS BORN, OKAY?
THAT'S WHAT OMASA SAYS, WITH SUCH A SEXY LOOK IN HER EYES!!
EH, WE DIDN'T WANT TO HEAR ABOUT THAT.
IN OTHER WORDS, THE BABY IS DOING FINE, RIGHT?
OF COURSE!
HE'S MY SON!!
WHAT MAKES YOU SAY THAT?
Son?

I'LL NEED A SON TO MAKE INTO A BUSHI!
THAT DOESN'T MEAN YOU'LL HAVE ONE.
BUT...
I SEE. OMASA-SAN...
SHE'S ONLY A YEAR OLDER THAN ME...
...BUT SHE'S ALREADY GOING TO BE A MOTHER ...
BUT I GUESS THAT'S TO BE EXPECTED AT 19 YEARS OLD.
A different time.
ARE YOU JEALOUS OF HER?

ARE YOU STUP—
O-OF COURSE NOT!!
BA-BUMP!
REALLY?
I'M SO ENVIOUS OF HARADA-SAN.
OH.
THAT'S RIGHT. HE'S TALKING ABOUT HARADA-SAN. WHAT AM I PANICKING FOR?
PHEW
PHEW
I'M GOING TO ASK HIM TO LET ME HOLD THE BABY!!
PLEASE CHANGE INTO YOUR KIMONO FIRST!!
OH, RIGHT.
HE'S SUCH A NUDIST.
OH.
YOUR NEW YUKATA LOOKS NICE!
IT LOOKS GREAT ON YOU.
DO YOU THINK SO?

SHWIP
?!
SHOCK
OH. VICE CAPTAIN?
!
DID I IMAGINE THAT?!
DAMN IT.
SOMETHING MUST BE WRONG WITH ME.
I'M SORRY. DID YOU NEED ME?
NO...
I'M GOING OUT FOR A WHILE.
I WON'T BE NEEDING COMPANY.

WHERE ARE YOU GOING?
DON'T EVEN ASK!
EAST OR WEST?
EAST.
GION...
VERY WELL. PLEASE ENJOY YOURSELF.
And it's still daytime, for God's sake...
HIJIKATA-SAAAAN. PLEASE ORDER ME TO COME WITH YOU!
IF IT'S FOR WORK IT WON'T BE CHEATING!!
I REFUSE!!
DRAG DRAG
I'M GLAD TO SEE THAT HIJIKATA-SAN...
...IS STARTING TO GET BACK TO HIS OLD SELF AGAIN.
AFTER ALL, HE'S BEEN DISTRACTED...
...EVER SINCE THAT INCIDENT WITH COUNCILOR ITO.
HE'D BEEN EXTREMELY ANXIOUS UP TO THAT POINT, SO PERHAPS IT WAS A REACTION TO THAT.

YOU GUUUYS ...
HAVE YOU BEEN STRANGELY INTIMATE THESE DAYS?
O-OF COURSE NOT!!
THEN LET ME FONDLE YOUR BOOBS, KAMIYA!!
THAT MAKES NO SENSE, HARADA-SAN!
WHY IS EVERY-ONE SO COLD TO ME?
I'M JUST A SAD, LONELY GUY!!
OKAY, OKAY. I GET IT!
I'LL GO WITH YOU TO SHIMABARA OR ANY OTHER PLACE YOU WANT TO GO!!
BUT I'M NOT INTERESTED IN GOING TO SHIMABARA...
C'mon, come closer.
PLEASE JOIN ME IN GOING TO SHIMABARA!

OKAAAY. YOU'RE LIKE A LITTLE BROTHER TO ME, SO I CAN'T TURN YOU DOWN, SOJI!
OKITA SENSEI?!
YOU DON'T NEED TO COME WITH US, KAMIYA-SAN.
WHO KNOWS ...
...WHAT HARADA-SAN IS CAPABLE OF IF HE GETS DRUNK.
...
HE PROTECTED ME.
Thanks a lot for treating me to this.
What? I'm paying?
OKITA SENSEI.
HE DIDN'T DO THAT BECAUSE I WOULD GET IN THE WAY OF THEIR FLIRTING, RIGHT?!
Hey!

IT'S ALMOST DARK BUT IT'S UNBE-LIEVABLY HOT.
...
THE BAKUFU AND CHOSHU ARMIES STILL HAVE THEIR SWORDS DRAWN ON ONE ANOTHER IN HIROSHIMA.
I HEAR THAT PRICES ARE RAPIDLY RISING IN EDO AND TARGETED PROTESTS HAVE BECOME MORE COMMON.
SO WHY IS KYOTO SO QUIET?
THIS UNUSUAL PEACE, AS IF THEY'RE ALL LEADING COSSETED LIVES...
...BOTHERS ME.

IS THIS THE CALM BEFORE THE STORM?
I SHOULD HURRY UP AND FINISH WHAT I CAME FOR.
MISS!
MISS!
I WILL DO THOSE CHORES. PLEASE DON'T GO OUTSIDE SO CARE-LESSLY!
WILL YOU CUT IT OUT, OCHIYO?!
STOP CALLING ME "MISS" AND CALL ME "MI-LADY."
HOW MANY TIMES DO I NEED TO TELL YOU THIS?!

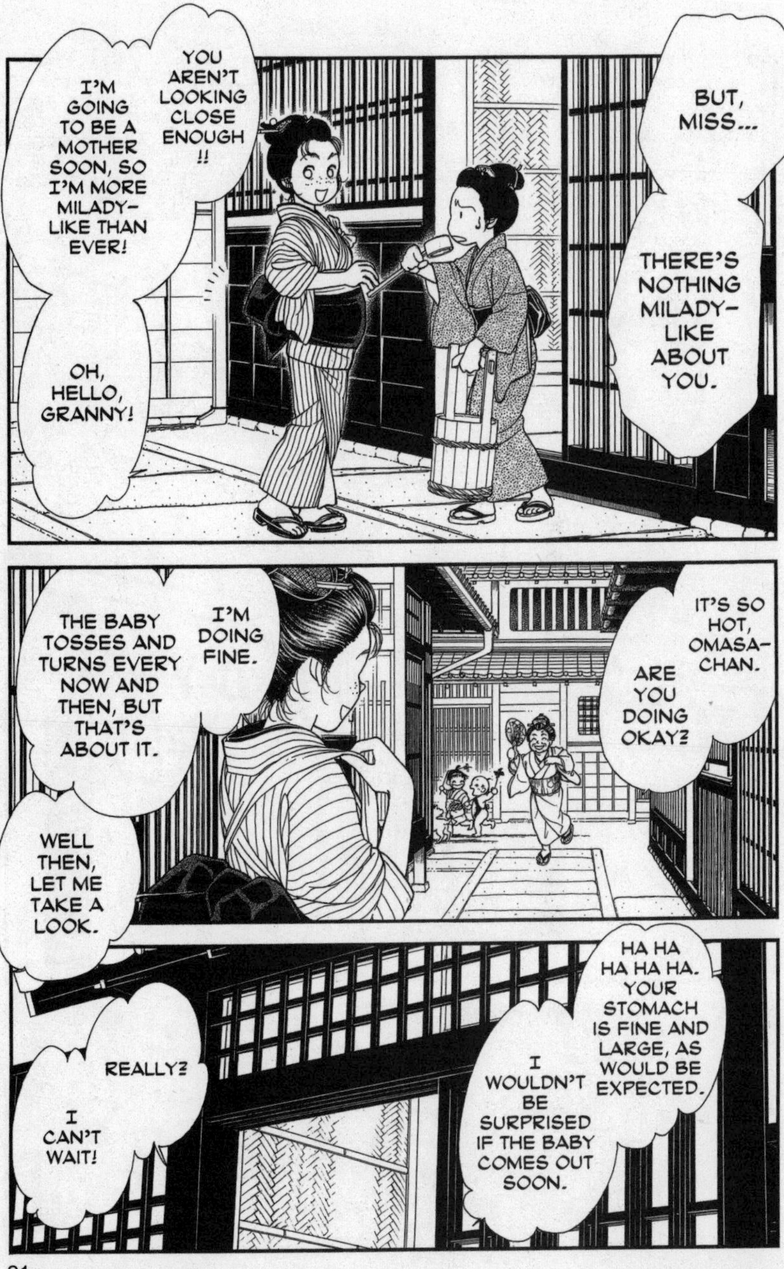
BUT, MISS...
THERE'S NOTHING MILADY-LIKE ABOUT YOU.
YOU AREN'T LOOKING CLOSE ENOUGH!!
I'M GOING TO BE A MOTHER SOON, SO I'M MORE MILADY-LIKE THAN EVER!
OH, HELLO, GRANNY!
IT'S SO HOT, OMASA-CHAN.
ARE YOU DOING OKAY?
I'M DOING FINE.
THE BABY TOSSES AND TURNS EVERY NOW AND THEN, BUT THAT'S ABOUT IT.
WELL THEN, LET ME TAKE A LOOK.
HA HA HA HA HA. YOUR STOMACH IS FINE AND LARGE, AS WOULD BE EXPECTED.
I WOULDN'T BE SURPRISED IF THE BABY COMES OUT SOON.
REALLY?
I CAN'T WAIT!

CALL FOR ME AS SOON AS YOU FEEL THE PANGS.
THIS WILL BE THE SEVENTH BABY I'VE HELPED OUT WITH, AND I'M AN EXPERT AT THIS!
RIGHT! I'M RELYING ON YOU, GRAN!
WHY DON'T YOU COME IN FOR SOME TEA...
THAT'S OKAY!
I'LL DROP BY AGAIN LATER. SAY HELLO TO YOUR HUSBAND FOR ME.
AH!
TRIP
GRANNY !!
OWWWW!
THIS ISN'T GOOD.
I'VE PUT OUT MY BAD BACK!
OCHIYO, GET A DOCTOR !!
YES!!

GRANNY, HOLD ON TO ME!
BA-BUMP!!
...!!
AH ...?
OMASA-CHAN, ARE YOU...?!
AAAAAAH!
WHAT SHOULD I DO, GRANNY?
THE BABY'S COMING OUT!!
OWWW.
HANG IN THERE, OMASA-CHAN!
OCHIYO-CHAN! OCHIYO-CHAN!
ANY-ONE! COME HELP!!

FOR GOD'S SAKE, ISN'T SANOSUKE HERE?!
INOUE SENSEI?
WHAT IS IT, GEN-SAN?
KONDO SENSEI!
WELL, FOR SOME CONVOLUTED REASON...
...SANO'S WIFE OMASA-SAN HAS SUDDENLY GONE INTO LABOR!
WHAAT?!
THE OLD MIDWIFE SHE'S GOT IS NO HELP AT ALL...
...AND I JUST HAPPENED TO RUN INTO ALL THE CHAOS WHEN I WAS MAKING MY ROUNDS!
HARADA SENSEI HAS GONE DOWN TO SHIMABARA WITH OKITA SENSEI!

TCH!
AT A TIME LIKE THIS? FOR GOD'S SAKE!
I'LL RUSH DOWN THERE RIGHT AWAY!
OKAY. THANKS, GEN-SAN!
CAP-TAIN!
I'LL GO AND HELP TOO!
WAIT, KAMIYA-KUN.
IF SHE WENT INTO LABOR AFTER AN ACCIDENT, THIS COULD END UP BEING A TROUBLESOME DELIVERY.
WOULDN'T IT BE BETTER IF WE ASKED MATSUMOTO HOGEN FOR ADVICE IN CASE SOME-THING HAPPENS?
YES...
THERE SHOULD BE OTHER MIDWIVES IN THE NEIGHBOR-HOOD.

THE WORST CASE SCENARIO WOULD BE IF THIS DOESN'T TURN OUT TO BE AN ORDINARY DELIVERY.
LIKE THE CAPTAIN SAID, UNCLE DROOPY-EYES SHOULD KNOW WHAT TO DO!
EXCUSE ME!
IS MATSUMO-TO HOGEN HOME?!
SHK
!!
KAMIYA?!
VICE CAP-TAIN?
DIDN'T YOU GO TO GION?

I-I JUST SAID I WAS GOING EAST!
HMM. WELL, THIS PLACE *IS* TO THE EAST OF OUR HEAD-QUARTERS...
BUT WHAT ARE YOU DOING HERE?
HE CAME TO TALK TO MACE, BUT...
WHAT? THEN IS HOGEN OUT TODAY, NANBU SENSEI?
YES. HE WENT TO OSAKA AGAIN.
TROUBLE WITH THE CHINESE MEDICINE DOCTORS AGAIN?
HOGEN OFTEN COMPLAINED THAT CHINESE MEDICINE PRACTITIONERS STILL CLAIM THEY ARE THE "TRUE PATH," AS PRIVATE DOCTORS OF THE BAKUFU.
ANYWAY, WHAT ARE *YOU* DOING HERE, KAMIYA?!
AH, RIGHT!! I CAME HERE FOR THE FOLLOWING REASON...
DON'T BE AN IDIOT!!
YOU CAN'T RELY ON THE SHOGUN'S PRIVATE DOCTOR FOR SOMETHING LIKE THAT!!
WHAT? BUT IT WAS THE CAPTAIN'S IDEA!

HUMPH. KAT-CHAN IS SUCH A SOFTY WITH HIS FRIENDS!!
IF YOU DON'T MIND, I WOULD BE WILLING TO HELP.
WHAT?!
YOU'RE BEING TOO KIND!! YOU'RE THE PRIVATE DOCTOR TO THE LORD OF AIZU YOURSELF, NANBU SENSEI...
...SO I CANNOT ALLOW YOU TO MAKE HOUSE CALLS TO COMMON PEOPLE...
YES, THOSE ARE THE RULES.
BUT THERE ARE WAYS TO GET AROUND THAT.
WHAT?! BUT...
WHO DO YOU THINK I AM?
I AM THE MACE'S DISCIPLE, YOU KNOW!
SHK
THANK YOU VERY MUCH, NANBU SENSEI...
AND AT A TIME LIKE THIS, TOO...

"I HAVE A QUESTION ABOUT KAMIYA'S ILLNESS.
"IS THERE A POSSIBILITY THAT HE IS *FEMALE BY NATURE* AND ONLY SEEMED MALE FOR A SHORT WHILE DUE TO HIS PHYSICAL GROWTH?"
"I'M SORRY, I AM NOT KNOWL-EDGEABLE ENOUGH ON THE MATTER OF FEMI-NINTITIS ..."
"I SEE... WHEN WILL HOGEN RETURN?"
"WELL..."
"PLEASE DON'T TELL THIS TO ANYONE BUT CAPTAIN KONDO ..."
COULD ...
...THE "STORM" BE ABOUT THIS?
VICE CAP-TAIN HIJI-KATA!!

I'LL ORDER A CARRIAGE FOR YOU IF YOU CAN'T KEEP UP WITH US!!
Why are you walking so slowly?!
D...
DON'T BE STUPID!!
SECOND YEAR OF KEIO, JUNE 7
(JULY 18, 1866)
THE BAKUFU SHIP THAT WAS INDECISIVE AT THE START OF THE BATTLE FINALLY OPENED FIRE ON THE CHOSHU ARMY AT SUO-OSHIMA.
THE SECOND CHOSHU EXPEDITION HAD BEGUN.

BUT...
OBVIOUSLY, NO ONE HERE WOULD HAVE HEARD NEWS OF THAT YET.
A DOCTOR ?!
GIVING BIRTH TO A BABY IS NOT AN ILLNESS!
ALL MEN OUT!!
BUT I'M THE HUSBAND !!
OH, KAMIYA-SAN.
AH, KAMIYA.
AH, KAMIYA.
TODO SENSEI, NAGAKURA SENSEI ?!
WHAT ARE YOU TWO DOING HERE?!
WE JUST HAPPENED TO BUMP INTO EACH OTHER AT SHIMABARA ...
...WHEN GEN-SAN APPEARED.
WHAT ?
YOU TOO, CAPTAIN ?!
WELL ...
I HAD TO COME AND SEE.

WOW.
THE WOMEN SURE ARE SOME-THING...
AAAAAH!
Omasa-chan!
Just a little more!
ALL THE WIVES FROM THE NEIGHBOR-HOOD GATHERED TO HELP...
...AND COM-PLETED THE PREPA-RATIONS...
...BEFORE WE COULD DO ANY-THING.
AAAAARGH!
Put your mind into it!!
BUT I GUESS THAT'S NATURAL.
...!
okay!
AFTER ALL, THOSE CRONES...
...HAVE ALL GIVEN BIRTH TO BABIES THEM-SELVES.
OHHHH!
You can do it!
BUT THEY ACT LIKE IT'S NOTHING...
THEY'RE ALL SO...
Come on!
AAAA

THIS IS HOW WE ARE ALL BORN...
WAAAAAAAAAAAAAH
!!
THE BABY'S BEEN BORN ...!!
HURRAY!!
AND AMIDST THE BEGINNING OF A RISING STORM...
...THE FIRST CHILD OF ASSISTANT VICE CAPTAIN HARADA SANOSUKE (27) OF THE TENTH TROOP WAS BORN.
GWAAAAH
GWAAAAH

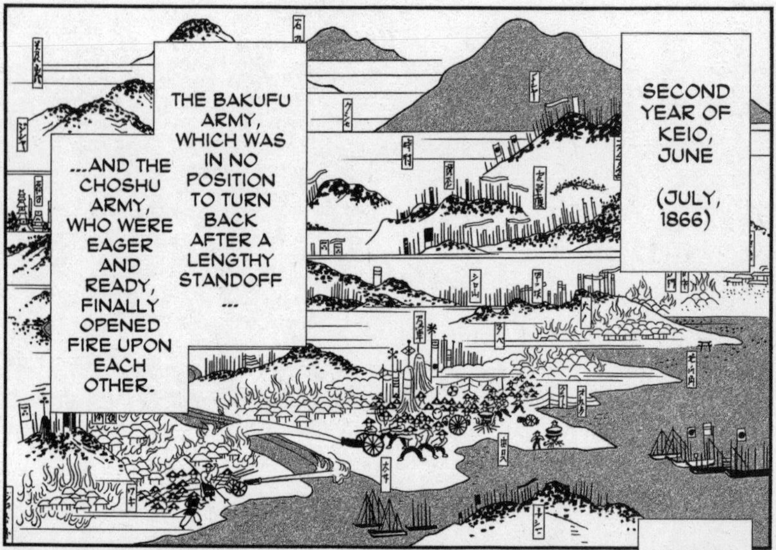

KAZE HIKARU SENRYU

...I WANT TO KILL
WITHOUT HESITATION
THE EGGHEAD

By
Mamezo-san
from
Okayama

THE FIRST CHILD OF HARADA SANOSUKE, ASSISTANT VICE CAPTAIN OF THE SHIN-SENGUMI'S TENTH TROOP...
...TURNED OUT TO BE A BOY, JUST AS HE HAD WISHED.
OOOH, HE'S SO CUTE. ♡
HA HA HA, DROOPY EYES!
RIGHT, DROOPY EYES.
DROOPY-EYED MONKEY.
GET OUT, ALL OF YOU!!
OOH, BUT THIS IS SO JOYOUS!
WE MUST THINK OF A GOOD NAME FOR HIM RIGHT AWAY!
OH, KONDO-SAN.
I'VE ALREADY THOUGHT OF THAT!

命名
茂
TA-DAH!
HIS NAME IS "SHIGERU" (茂)!!
"SHIGE-RU" (茂)?!
SANO-SUKE, WAIT.
YOU DIDN'T ...
THAT'S RIGHT!
I BORROWED A LETTER FROM OUR SHOGUN, LORD IEMOCHI (家茂)!!
ARE YOU AN IDIOT?!
YOU ARE BEING TOO PRESUMPTUOUS, HARADA SENSEI!!!
NAMES LIKE THAT ARE BESTOWED BY THE SHOGUN WHEN YOU DISTINGUISH YOURSELF IN WAR!!
YOU KNOW THAT!!
BUT THE SWEET-SAKE SELLER WHO DROPS BY NISHI HONGANJI A LOT...
HIS NAME IS "MOKICHI" (茂吉), RIGHT?
IF A SWEET-SAKE SELLER CAN USE THAT KANJI, SO CAN MY SON.
MOKICHI IS A 50-YEAR-OLD COOT!!
HE HAS NOTHING TO DO WITH LORD IEMOCHI!!

COME ON, THINK IT OVER.
BORROW A KANJI FROM KONDO SENSEI, SANO-SUKE!
KONDO-SAN ONLY HAS "ISAMI" (勇) IN HIS NAME.
THEN...
...SOMETHING LIKE "YUNO-SUKE" (勇之助) OR "YUZA-BURO" (勇三郎).
I WANT HIM TO HAVE A ONE-LETTER NAME!
IN THAT WAY, I WANT TO FOLLOW KONDO-SAN AS AN EXAMPLE.
NO ONE IS AS LUCKY AS HIM!
Me?!
NOW THAT YOU MENTION IT...
...YOU ARE RIGHT!
Right.
BORN AS THE SON OF A PEASANT AND NOW THE CAPTAIN OF THE SHIN-SENGUMI...
HE MAY EVEN BECOME A DAIMYO ONE DAY. A LITTLE WHILE AGO, WE WEREN'T EVEN ALLOWED TO HAVE THAT DREAM.
I STILL CAN'T ALLOW IT!
YOU CAN'T USE THAT NAME, SANO-SUKE!!

HIJI-KATA-SAN?
WHAT IF BAD LUCK STRIKES THE SHOGUN...
...AFTER YOU MAKE A RASH DECISION LIKE THAT?!
YOUR SON WILL BE BRANDED WITH A BAD NAME FOR LIFE!
IT'S NOT LIKE YOU...
...TO WORRY ABOUT SOME-THING BAD THAT HASN'T EVEN HAP-PENED, HIJIKATA-SAN.
...!
GASP
IF YOU THINK SOMETHING BAD IS GOING TO HAPPEN, THAT IS ALL THE MORE REASON FOR ME TO RAISE HIM TO BECOME A FINE BUSHI THAT CAN PROTECT HIM!
RIGHT, SHIGERU?!
YOU HAVE BEEN GIVEN LORD IEMOCHI'S NAME AS AN ADVANCE PAYMENT.
HA HA HA.
YOU'RE AN INTER-ESTING MAN AS ALWAYS, SANOSUKE!
SO YOU HAVE TO MAKE A NAME FOR YOURSELF IN WAR!

*Children were birthed from a sitting position back then, and the mother was not supposed to lie down until the seventh day after birth in order to avoid disease.

"MACE IS IN OSAKA."
"HE MAY NOT SEEM LIKE IT, BUT HE IS THE PRIVATE DOCTOR OF THE SHOGUN.
"THE CHINESE MEDICINE DOCTORS MAY NOT LIKE HIM ...
"...BUT HE DOESN'T HAVE TIME TO PLAY AROUND IN KYOTO ..."
"DOES THAT MEAN ..."
"...SOMETHING THE CHINESE MEDICINE DOCTORS CAN'T DEAL WITH...
...HAS OCCURRED?"
"THERE'S NO OUTSMARTING YOU, IS THERE?
"I'M WORRIED THAT IT WOULD CAUSE GREATER WORRY IF I LIED TO YOU ABOUT IT."

"PLEASE DON'T TELL THIS TO ANYONE EXCEPT CAPTAIN KONDO..."
I CAN'T EVEN TELL KONDO-SAN ABOUT IT.
IT WOULD ONLY BE ANOTHER HEAD-ACHE HE DOESN'T NEED.
IS THERE SOMETHING YOU ARE WORRIED ABOUT?
SHOCK
W-WHAT?!
WHAT DO YOU WANT, KAMIYA?
HAVE YOU FOR-GOTTEN?
WITH ALL DUE RESPECT ...
...I AM YOUR KOSHO, VICE CAPTAIN.

IT IS EXTREMELY ANNOYING TO SEE YOU GET SO IRRITATED EVERY TIME I'M NEAR!
HE IS SO ANNOYING ...!!
WELL, I'M SORRY!
I WAS DEEP IN THOUGHT ABOUT A HAIKU I'M WORKING ON, SO YOU SURPRISED ME!
OH.
WHAT KIND OF HAIKU IS IT?
POP
W-WHAT ARE YOU DOING HERE, SOJI?!
WELL...
I WENT OUT TO TAKE A LEAK WHEN I NOTICED YOU TWO HAPPILY CHATTING.
WHAT?!
HAPPILY?!
SEE? YOU TWO GET ALONG SO WELL.

ARE YOU...
...KIDDING ME?!
...KIDDING ME?!
WHY WOULD I...?!
WOW, YOU SOUND LIKE TWINS!! ♥
VICE CAPTAIN HIJIKATA!
WE RECEIVED A MESSAGE FROM AIZU HAN...
SAITO SENSEI.
WHAT HAPPENED?!
THE LAST SEVENTH...
...AT SUO-OSHIMA...
THE BAKUFU ARMY HAS OPENED FIRE AGAINST CHOSHU!
WAR?!

OOOOH, WAR HAS BROKEN OUT!!
LET'S GET READY AND GO!!
WE'RE GONNA ATTACK CHOSHU AS WELL!!
EEEEK!
PLEASE LET GO OF THE BABY!!
OOH, OCHIYO! SHIGERU IS A LUCKY GUY!
DADDY HAS BEEN GIVEN THE OPPOR-TUNITY TO MAKE A NAME FOR HIMSELF!!
GWAAAAH
GWAAAAH
WHAAAAAAAT?!
EH, I'M SORRY TO DISAPPOINT YOU...
...BUT THE SHINSENGUMI HAS NOT RECEIVED ORDERS TO SEND OUR MEN.
ISN'T IT OBVIOUS?!
OUR DUTY IS TO MAINTAIN THE SECURITY OF KYOTO!

THAT'S BORING, CAPTAIN!
UM...
LET'S VOLUNTEER TO FIGHT IN THE WAR!
I UNDERSTAND HOW YOU FEEL...
BUT YOU MUSTN'T BE SO DISCOURTEOUS!
IF WE DO NOT STAY HERE, WHO WILL PROTECT THE EMPEROR AND SHOGUN...
...IF THE CHOSHU ARMY MANAGES TO ATTACK KYOTO?!
COUNCILOR ITO...!
THEN...
IS THAT WHY THE LORD OF AIZU LEFT US IN KYOTO?!
OH?
DID YOU THINK IT WAS BECAUSE HE DID NOT TRUST US, CAPTAIN?
YES!
I HAVE BEEN FILLED WITH REGRET AT NOT BEING ABLE TO BE OF ANY HELP BACK IN HIROSHIMA...
ABSURD.
IT'S QUITE THE OPPOSITE!

THANK YOU VERY MUCH, COUNCILOR ITO!
I WAS ALMOST UNDER THE WRONG IMPRESSION!
WE HAVE NO TIME TO LOSE!
TOSHI! LET'S HOLD A MEETING !!
HA HA HA ...
OUR KONDO ISAMI ...
...IS SO CUTE, ISN'T HE?
HEH
BA-BUMP
WHAT ...
what is with that smile ?!

Tsundere is a term that refers to characters who are cold in the beginning but become loving once they open up. "Dere-tsun" is a humorous reversal of that concept. –Ed.

HIJIKATA-SAN CAN'T DENY THAT...
...AND THAT IRRITATES HIM EVEN MORE. ♡
HIJIKATA-SAN IS SO UNYIELDING, ISN'T HE? ♡
BY THE WAY, DON'T YOU HAVE SOME TASKS TO COMPLETE FOR THE MEETING, LITTLE KOSHO?
YES. THEY GAVE ME THE COLD SHOULDER AGAIN.
OKITA SENSEI... I GET THE IMPRESSION EVERY NOW AND THEN THAT YOU'RE PRETTY SIMILAR TO THE COUNCILOR.
In other words, a weirdo.
SENSEI... WHEN WILL I BE GIVEN PERMISSION TO RETURN TO THE FIRST TROOP?
WHAT?!
OHHH...
MY WOUNDED SHOULDER HAS ALREADY HEALED.
VICE CAPTAIN HIJIKATA IS BACK TO HIS USUAL SELF TOO...
DOES HE STILL NEED ME AROUND?

WELL, YOU ARE A VERY HANDY PERSON TO HAVE AROUND, KAMIYA-SAN.
THE VICE CAPTAIN PROBABLY FEELS THE SAME WAY, AND IT MUST BE DIFFICULT FOR HIM TO CONSIDER PARTING WITH YOU.
BUT HE ALWAYS TOSSES ME ASIDE AS IF I'M IN HIS WAY!!
WHEN I'M ALONE WITH HIM AT NIGHT, WE HAVE NOTHING TO TALK ABOUT.
I MISS THE CHEERFUL AND ROWDY NIGHTS WITH THE FIRST TROOP...
HA HA HA.
RIGHT. NOW THAT I REMEMBER IT, WE USED TO...
!!
often slept like this.
I-I WONDER HOW I EVEN MANAGED TO SLEEP IN THAT SITUATION?!
ACTU-ALLY!!
I-I THINK IT IS BETTER FOR YOU THIS WAY.
ALSO, THE TROOP'S ROOM STINKS DURING SUMMER!

YOU'RE TELLING ME THAT NOW?
I'VE GOTTEN USED TO IT ALREADY.
YES, BUT I-I STILL THINK ...
...IT IS A LOT SAFER IN MANY WAYS...
...FOR YOU TO REMAIN A KOSHO!
WHAT DO YOU MEAN?
I DIDN'T WANT TO TELL YOU THIS, BUT... WELL...
KAMIYA-SAN...
YOUR BODY IS BECOMING MORE ROUNDED AND WOMANLY ...
WHAT ?!
WHEN DID YOU SEE IT?!
The bath?!
I HAVEN'T SEEN IT!!
I HAVEN'T, BUT I CAN STILL TELL!
L-LIKE WHEN YOU GRAB ONTO ME!!
...!!

IT'S BECAUSE I HAVEN'T BEEN TRAINING ENOUGH!!
I'M SORRY!!
I'LL TRAIN SO HARD THAT MY ARMS AND LEGS WILL GET THICKER THAN YOURS!!
WHAT?
THAT'S YOUR SOLUTION?!
HOW CARELESS COULD I HAVE BEEN?!
HOW COULD I HAVE THE NERVE TO DEMAND TO GO BACK TO THE FIRST TROOP WITHOUT CONSIDERING HOW LAZY I'VE BEEN?!
YOU SHOULD BE ASHAMED OF YOURSELF, SEIZABURO!!
I WILL START TRAINING RIGOROUSLY THIS VERY MINUTE!!
IF I MAY GIVE YOU MY HONEST OPINION—

THIS EXPEDITION...
...WILL PROBABLY END WITH THE BAKUFU'S REPUTATION BEING CRUSHED TO SMITHEREENS.
AND THAT WOULD BE THE BEST OUTCOME.
THERE IS A GOOD POSSIBILITY...
...THAT THE CHOSHU ARMY WILL GATHER MOMENTUM AND MARCH RIGHT UP TO KYOTO...
...WHILE JOINING HANDS WITH THE NUMEROUS HANS WHO UNTIL NOW HAVE BEEN WATCHING AND WAITING.
AND THE ONLY POSSIBILITY OF STOPPING THAT...
...WOULD BE IF THE SHOGUN HIMSELF WERE TO MAKE AN APPEARANCE...
...AND INSPIRE THE UNDISCIPLINED BAKUFU ARMY!
BUT THAT WOULD BE IMPOSSIBLE!
THE SHOGUN WOULD NEVER APPEAR AT AN EXPEDITION AGAINST A SINGLE HAN LIKE CHOSHU...

THE BAKUFU ARMY WILL LOSE?!
EVEN SO...
IT WOULD STILL BE BENEFICIAL FOR YOU TO GIVE THAT ADVICE.
AFTER ALL, PEOPLE WILL HOLD YOU IN HIGH ESTEEM LATER ON...
...WHEN THEY'RE THINKING, "IF ONLY WE HAD ACCEPTED KONDO'S ADVICE BACK THEN"...
THAT MEANS NOTHING.
WHY DO YOU SAY THAT, HIJIKATA-KUN?
WHAT POINT IS THERE IN MAKING A NAME FOR ONESELF AFTER THE BAKUFU HAS BEEN DEFEATED?
WE WOULD GIVE NO CARE TO SELF-PRESERVATION IN A SITUATION LIKE THAT.
IN THAT CASE, YOU SHOULD IMMEDIATELY GO AND MEET THE LORD OF AIZU!
NO, GO TO OSAKA CASTLE, WHERE THE SHOGUN RESIDES!
PLEAD WITH HIM TO GIVE THE ORDER FOR THE SHINSEN-GUMI TO PARTICIPATE IN THE WAR!!
誠
THAT IS IMPOSSIBLE!!

TOSHI ...
IS THERE SOME-THING YOU KNOW?
...
THIS IS TOP SECRET EVEN AMONG THE BAKUFU...
...BUT THE SHOGUN ...
...IS ILL RIGHT NOW.
WHAT ...?!
ACCORD-ING TO NANBU SENSEI ...
...THE SHOGUN IS A VERY ROBUST PERSON ...
...SO HE SHOULD RECOVER SOON.
MATSUMOTO HOGEN HAS ALSO BEEN SUMMONED TO PROVIDE MEDICAL CARE...
...AND IS CURRENTLY RESIDING AT OSAKA CASTLE.
AND?! WHAT IS THE SHOGUN'S ILLNESS?

I HAVE BEEN TOLD IT IS THE EDO DISEASE.
BERIBERI ?!
BERIBERI WAS POPULARLY CALLED THE EDO DISEASE BECAUSE IT WAS A RECURRING ILLNESS IN EDO...
... WHERE THE STAPLE FOOD WAS WHITE RICE.
IT WAS ALSO WELL KNOWN FOR BEING THE ILLNESS THAT TOOK THE LIFE OF THE PREVIOUS SHOGUN, IESADA.
IT FREQUENTLY MANIFESTS AS A CASE OF NEURITIS, WHICH BEGINS WITH PARALYSIS OF THE LEGS.
BUT IF THE NEURITIS REACHES THE HEART, IT CAN END IN HEART FAILURE AND DEATH.
LAST AUTUMN ...
...WE WENT TO FUSHIMI UNDER THE ORDERS OF HIGO-SAMA ...
...TO STOP THE SHOGUN FROM RESIGNING FROM HIS DUTIES.
LORD IEMOCHI ...?!

IS THAT YOU, KAMIYA ?!
I-I'M VERY SORRY!!
I CAME TO GET MY BELONGINGS FROM YOUR ROOM...
...AND OVER-HEARD THE CONVER-SATION!
TCH!
I AM SURE YOU ARE QUITE AWARE ---
...THAT YOU MUST KEEP THIS A SECRET EVEN IF IT COSTS YOU YOUR LIFE!!
IF THIS NEWS GOES PUBLIC ---
...THE BAKUFU ARMY MAY WELL FALL APART...
...IN THE MIDDLE OF THE EXPEDITION.
YES! I WILL PROTECT THE SECRET WITH MY LIFE!!
KA-MIYA-KUN...

TELL ME...
IS THE EDO DISEASE...
IS BERI-BERI...
...A LIFE-THREAT-ENING ILLNESS?
NO, CAPTAIN!!
I KNOW OF MANY CASES IN WHICH THE PATIENT RECOVERED!!
AND MATSUMOTO HOGEN HIMSELF IS TREATING THE SHOGUN...
...SO YOU MAY REST ASSURED...
...THAT HE WILL RECOVER!
I SEE.
SIGH
IS THAT SO...
YES!
THE SUMMER HEAT MUST HAVE INFLAMED THE BERIBERI.
BUT THE SHOGUN IS STILL YOUNG.
I AM SURE HE WILL BE BETTER BY AUTUMN!

AH, I SEE.
THANK YOU, KAMIYA-KUN!
I FEEL VERY RELIEVED.
I'M GLAD YOU WERE EAVES-DROPPING ON US!
HA HA HA...
IT IS AN HONOR!
...

GOOD WORK ... ...JUST NOW.
VICE CAP-TAIN.
THE ILLNESS IS PROBABLY NOT THAT SIMPLE...
...BUT IT WON'T DO ANY GOOD TO GIVE THE CAPTAIN BAD NEWS.
SO, THANKS.
VICE CAP-TAIN ...
Um..
WILL ...
WILL THE SHOGUN BE ALL RIGHT?
THE FACT THAT HOGEN HAS BEEN SUM-MONED ...
...MEANS THE ILLNESS IS BEYOND WHAT THE CHINESE MEDICINE PRACTI-TIONERS CAN HANDLE!
TCH!
YOU'RE SUCH A CRYBABY!

BUT I APPLAUD YOU FOR NOT CRYING IN FRONT OF THE CAPTAIN.
THE ONLY THING WE CAN DO NOW IS...
...TRUST IN MATSU-MOTO HOGEN AND CARRY OUT OUR OWN DUTIES.
YES ...
...
WHOOSH

OSAKA CASTLE
WHSHHH
I DON'T LIKE IT WHEN THE WIND BLOWS...
MY LORD.
IT IS TIME FOR YOUR EVENING EXAMI- NATION.
AH... YOU'RE IN CHARGE TONIGHT, MATSU- MOTO...
VERY WELL.
YOU MAY AP- PROACH ME.

HOW ARE YOU FEELING ...
MY LORD?
DON'T WORRY ...
I ATE SOME CASTELLA TODAY.
IS THAT SO?

KAZE HIKARU SENRYU
I WON'T BE YOUR "BIG BROTHER" FOREVER
By Kurosuke-san from Okayama

IT SEEMS AS THOUGH EVERYONE KNOWS I HAVE A SWEET TOOTH...
PEOPLE HAVE BEEN SENDING ME ALL MANNER OF SWEETS ...
HOW KIND OF THEM.
YES...
EVERYONE CARES DEEPLY FOR YOUR HEALTH AND WELL-BEING.
YOU MUST FULLY RECOVER AS SOON AS YOU CAN, MY LORD.
HMM ...
YOU'RE RIGHT...
I HAVE ...
...BEEN WORRYING MIYA SO MUCH...
I WANT TO RELIEVE HER OF HER WORRIES...
YES, MY LORD.
"MIYA" ...

...REFERS TO KAZUNOMIYA, THE WIFE OF SHOGUN IEMOCHI ...
...AND THE YOUNG SISTER OF THE CURRENT EMPEROR KOMEI.
SHE FELL VICTIM TO THE UNION OF THE IMPERIAL COURT AND THE SHOGUNATE WHEN SHE WAS SEPARATED FROM THE FIANCÉ TO WHOM SHE HAD BEEN ENGAGED SINCE CHILDHOOD IN ORDER TO MARRY IEMOCHI.
AT THE TIME, THE PUBLIC SAW HER AS A TRAGIC PRINCESS.
BOTH SHE AND IEMOCHI WERE 17 YEARS OLD WHEN THEY MET.
SHE GRADUALLY OPENED UP TO IEMOCHI, WHO WAS SINCERE AND CARING...
...AND TOGETHER THEY BUILT A TRULY HARMONIOUS RELATIONSHIP.
WHAT DO YOU THINK, MATSUMOTO HOGEN?!
CHIEF WESTERN MEDICINE DOCTOR: TAKENOUCHI GENDO HOIN

*A disease that causes pain and inflammation in the muscles and joints. Rheumatic fever also causes endocarditis.

THEY'RE SUCH OUTDATED IDIOTS!!
TAKE-NOUCHI HOIN.
I UNDER-STAND HOW YOU FEEL...
BUT OUR TOP PRIORITY IS TO RELIEVE THE DISCOMFORT OUR LORD IS EXPERIENCING.
IF WE, THE PRIVATE DOCTORS, KEEP BICKERING WITH ONE ANOTHER ABOUT RHEUMATISM THIS AND BERIBERI THAT, IT WILL ONLY WORRY HIM EVEN MORE.
I AM WELL AWARE OF THAT!!
WE JUST WANT TO HELP THE SHOGUN!
BUT...
...EVEN LADY KAZUNOMIYA IN EDO KEEPS SENDING CHINESE MEDICINE DOCTORS DOWN TO OSAKA CASTLE!
IT IS AS IF THEY ARE IMPLYING THAT WE WESTERN MEDICINE DOCTORS ARE USELESS!!
HOIN...
AAAAH, WHAT A PAIN IN THE NECK!

THE PRIVATE DOCTORS ARE TOO PROUD.
THE HUMAN RELATION-SHIPS AT STAKE ARE FAR MORE AGGRAVATING TO ME THAN ANYTHING ELSE.
THE SHOGUN SMILED AT ME...
...TO TRY AND RELIEVE ME OF MY WORRIES, EVEN THOUGH HE COULD NOT BREATHE CLEARLY.
HE SHOWED HIS GRATITUDE TOWARD OTHERS EVEN IN HIS UN-FORTUNATE SITUATION...
AND HOW PUREHEARTED HE WAS TO EXHIBIT HIS DEEP CONCERN FOR LADY KAZUNOMIYA.
HE IS A TREASURE TO THE TOKUGAWA SHOGU-NATE.
I HAVE TO PROTECT HIM, NO MATTER WHAT!!

YOU CAN DO IT, UNCLE DROOPY EYES!!
WE WILL PLEDGE ON OUR LIVES...
...TO PERFORM OUR DUTIES TO THE BEST OF OUR ABILITIES!!
BASH
NOT THAT THERE IS ANYTHING MUCH TO DO AS THE VICE CAPTAIN'S KOSHO!!
BASH BASH
KRAK
AAAH! VERY WELL, KAMIYA! JUST SHUT UP!!

WHAT? I HAVEN'T SAID ANYTHING!
I CAN SMELL IT EMANATING FROM YOUR BODY!!
THE ROTTEN STENCH OF YOU COMPLAINING, "I'M BORED! I'M BORED!"
HOW RUDE! DON'T SPEAK OF ME LIKE SOME ROTTING CORPSE!
JUST GO AND PARTICIPATE IN THE FIRST TROOP'S ROUNDS FOR THE REST OF THE DAY.
ARE YOU SURE ABOUT THAT, VICE CAPTAIN HIJIKATA, SIR?!
SITTING UP!
DON'T SUDDENLY ACT ALL GRATEFUL.
I'M ONLY TELLING YOU TO GET OUT BECAUSE YOU STINK!
OOOH. "YOU'RE SO BASHFUL."
A-BUMP

YOU WANT ME TO SLICE YOU DOWN TO SIZE?!
DON'T EVER MIMIC THE WAY ITO SPEAKS AGAIN!!
YEEES.
I'LL BE GOING, THEN!!
HMPH!
OKITA SENSEI!!
WHAT...?

HUGGG
OKITA SENSEI!!
I, KAMIYA, WILL BE RETURNING TO FIRST TROOP DUTIES FOR ONE DAY!!
WHAAAAAAT?!
REALLY, KAMIYA?!
I'M SO GLAD! HOW MANY MONTHS HAS IT BEEN?!!
BUT...
W...
WHY?!
ORDERS FROM THE VICE CAPTAIN!
HE SAID THE ROOMS STINKS WHEN I'M AROUND.
"STINKS"? SHOULDN'T THAT BE "SMELLS GOOD"?
HAS THE VICE CAPTAIN FINALLY SURRENDERED TO KAMIYA'S ALLURE TOO?
...!

THE VICE CAPTAIN CAN BE SO THOUGHTLESS.
IT'S NOTHING BUT A NUISANCE TO HAVE SOMEONE WHO'S BEEN DOING DESK WORK FOR HALF A YEAR SUDDENLY RETURN.
WHAT ...
I'LL ABANDON YOU IF YOU CANNOT KEEP UP WITH US...
PLEASE REMEMBER THAT, KAMIYA-SAN.
OF COURSE !!
HOW TOUGH COULD IT BE?
AFTER ALL, I GET TO TAKE PART IN TROOP DUTIES SIDE BY SIDE WITH OKITA SENSEI!

HEY.
ISN'T OKITA SENSEI WALKING STRANGELY FAST TODAY?
TMP TMP TMP TMP TMP
FOR GOD'S SAKE ...
HE GETS SO STRICT WHEN KAMIYA IS AROUND.
IT'S SO HOT ...
HAA
WHAT'S WRONG?
GIVING UP ALREADY?
HAA

ARE YOU KIDDING?
I'M ONLY GETTING STARTED!
I'M GLAD TO HEAR THAT.
SMILE
ONI-IIII!!
TMP TMP
TMP TMP
TMP
IS IT LOVE...?
IT'S LOVE...
SEVEN MILLION RYO?!
THAT'S RIGHT.
THE BAKUFU CLAIMED IT WAS FOR WAR FUNDS FOR THE CHOSHU EXPEDITION...
...AND REQUESTED THE TOWNSPEOPLE IN OSAKA, HYOGO AND NISHINOMIYA HAND OVER THAT AMOUNT!
SHH!
NO WONDER PEOPLE ARE PROTESTING!

*Another moniker for the Shogun.

HAS...
...SOME-THING HAP-PENED?
"KEEP IT A SECRET EVEN IF IT COSTS YOU YOUR LIFE!!"
OH... UM...
UM...
I'M SORRY.
I CANNOT TELL YOU!
...
THAT'S WHAT I THOUGHT...
HEH
WHAT?

YOU ARE THE VICE CAPTAIN'S KOSHO ...
...SO IT'S ONLY NATURAL YOU WOULD HAVE SECRETS THAT YOU CANNOT SPEAK OF.
THERE IS NO REASON FOR YOU TO APOLOGIZE.
Y... ES...
THANK YOU VERY MUCH...
OKITA SENSEI ...
... DOESN'T MIND.
BUT I HATE IT.
I DON'T WANT MORE SECRETS BETWEEN OKITA SENSEI AND ME.
IT'S PART OF MY WORK, SO I UNDER-STAND...
...AND I KNOW I'M BEING TOO SOFT...
...BUT I CAN'T HELP FEELING THAT WAY.

I WANT TO GO BACK TO THE FIRST TROOP!!
WHAT IS WRONG WITH YOU NOW?!
THIS TIME YOU SERIOUSLY STINK!!
OH?
MAYBE YOU WANT ME TO SLEEP ELSEWHERE TONIGHT?
THAT IS UNNECESSARY!
AND GET RID OF THE SOURCE OF THAT RANCID SMELL—I KNOW YOU'RE HIDING IT!!
HIDING?
WHAT ARE YOU TALKING ABOUT?
DON'T PLAY DUMB WITH ME!!
YOU'RE HIDING A ROTTEN MACKEREL OR SOMETHING, AREN'T YOU?!
DON'T TOUCH MY BREASTS!!
I'LL SCREAM AND SAY YOU TRIED TO FORCE YOURSELF UPON ME!!
MAY I COME IN...
...VICE CAPTAIN HIJIKATA?

She really was hiding something rotten...

THAT BRAT.
HE'S DYING TO RETURN TO THE FIRST TROOP, YOU KNOW.
IT'S NOT LIKE THAT.
BY THE WAY, VICE CAPTAIN, THIS SEEMS TO BE A REPORT FROM INVESTIGATOR YAMAZAKI IN HIROSHIMA.
...
ARE THEY IDIOTS?!
WHY IS THE BAKUFU ARMY SO STUPID?!
YOU'RE RAISING YOUR VOICE, VICE CAPTAIN.
THE CHOSHU EXPEDITION BY THE BAKUFU...
...WAS STATIONED ALONG THE BORDER OF THE FOUR HANS THAT SURROUNDED CHOSHU, WHICH WERE...
...GEISHU (HIROSHIMA HAN), SEKISHU (TSUWANO HAN), SUO-OSHIMA (IWAKUNI HAN) AND KOKURA (KOKURA HAN).
Sekishu Border
Kokura Border
Geishu Border
Oshima Border
GEISHU, WHICH WAS THE FRONTLINE OF THE BAKUFU ARMY'S ATTACK, WOULD HAVE BEEN THE MOST ADVANTAGEOUS BATTLEFIELD FOR THEM...

...BUT THE UNDIS-CIPLINED ALLIED FORCES OF THE BAKUFU...
...GOT INTO A SQUABBLE WITH THE SAKAKIBARA ARMY (TAKADA HAN) AND THE II ARMY (HIKONE HAN), WITH EACH SIDE TRYING TO TAKE CHARGE OF THE MARCH...
...WHICH ENDED WITH THE DEFEAT OF BOTH FACTIONS BEFORE THEY COULD LEARN TO COOPERATE.
YOU'VE GOT TO BE KIDDING.
IF WORD OF THIS REACHES THE EARS OF THE SH...
VICE CAPTAIN!
DO I STILL SMELL?!
WHAT? OH.
It's a secret, right?!
I THINK IT'S FINE.
Sorry, Kamiya.
WELL, THEN.
I WILL BE LEAVING.

WHAT ...?
SHK
WAS HE LAUGHING AT ME AGAIN?!
"IT'S SO NICE TO SEE THEM GETTING ALONG"...
I HOPE HE WASN'T THINKING THAT!!
YOU'RE ...
...SO FUN TO WATCH, KAMIYA ...
Especially your face.
...
THE MOON ...

DAMN MOON.
LOOKING SO NON-CHALANT.
WHY ISN'T IT GETTING COOLER AT NIGHT?!
IT LOOKS JUST LIKE ... ... KAMIYA-SAN'S SULKY FACE...
THE EXTREME HEAT THAT SUMMER ONLY CAUSED MORE MISERY FOR IEMOCHI, WHO WAS BEDRIDDEN AT OSAKA CASTLE.
THE DEDICATED CARE OF THE PRIVATE DOCTORS PROVED UNSUCCESSFUL AS THE DAYS PASSED.
I HEAR...
...THAT YOU ARE ON GOOD TERMS WITH THE SHINSEN-GUMI.
IS THAT TRUE, MATSU-MOTO?

*The Lord of Aizu, Matsudaira Higonokami Katamori.

BUT WHEN I MADE UP MY MIND TO MEET HIM, HE TURNED OUT TO BE A FINE, VERY COURTEOUS MAN.
HE TOLD ME THAT HE WANTED TO STUDY UNDER ME AS I WAS SOMEONE WHO WAS ACQUAINTED WITH WESTERN WAYS OF THINKING.
I WAS DEEPLY TOUCHED BY KONDO'S SINCERE PASSION AND LOVE FOR THIS COUNTRY ...
...AND WE HAVE HAD A CLOSE RELATIONSHIP SINCE THEN.
HA HA...
I HAVE HEARD STORIES ABOUT YOUR UNUSUAL COURAGE ...
...SO I AM SURE YOU TWO MUST GET ALONG WELL.
IS IT TRUE THAT YOU USED A DANGEROUS DRUG IN ORDER TO CURE ...
...HITOTSUBASHI'S INTRACTABLE BRAIN CONGESTION, AND CAUSED HIS RECOVERY?
I'M SORRY !!
I RISKED HAVING TO COMMIT SEPPUKU WHEN I CHOSE TO TREAT HIM THAT WAY.
FWIP
THAT IS WHY ...
... PEOPLE TRUST YOU...
YOU ARE VERY...
... RELIABLE...

CHI... KA...
...
HE HAS FINALLY GONE TO SLEEP.
HE'S HAD VERY LITTLE SLEEP THESE DAYS.
PLEASE MAKE SURE HE IS NOT DIS-TURBED.
HE MUTTERED "CHI-KA" ...
YES!
WHAT WAS HE TRYING TO SAY?
AH, MATSU-MOTO HOGEN.
WE WOULD VERY MUCH LIKE TO MEET OUR LORD RIGHT AWAY...

CHIEF ELDER: ITAKURA IGANOKAMI
WILL ALL DUE RESPECT, IGANOKAMI-SAMA, PLEASE WAIT UNTIL TOMORROW MORNING.
OUR LORD HAS FINALLY MANAGED TO FALL ASLEEP.
ELDER: OGASAWARA IKINOKAMI
THIS IS A MATTER OF NATIONAL EMERGENCY!!
HE WILL HAVE TO WAKE UP!!
THIS IS TOP SECRET, SO WE NEED TO ASK YOU TO LEAVE, MATSUMOTO!
YES SIR!
HA!
POMPOUS OGASAWARA, THICK-HEADED-KAMI!!
HE WAS ORDERED TO GO DOWN TO CHUGOKU AND KYUSHU TO CHECK ON THE EXPEDITION ...
...BUT ONLY HAS THE BRAINS TO BRAG ABOUT THE SOUVENIRS HE BROUGHT BACK FROM NAGASAKI!
THE WORLD'S FALLING APART BECAUSE PEOPLE LIKE YOU ARE ELDERS!!
These kinds of complaints lead to people's dislike of him.

BUT WHAT MY LORD NEEDS RIGHT NOW IS PEACE AND COMFORT.
IF POSSIBLE, I WOULD LIKE TO SEND HIM BACK TO EDO...
...WHERE HE WILL BE ABLE TO REST WITH LADY KAZUNOMIYA IN PEACE.
BUT IF THE SHOGUN WERE TO LEAVE OSAKA CASTLE NOW...
...IT WOULD SEEM AS THOUGH HE WERE ABANDONING HIS DUTIES AS LEADER.
POOR SHOGUN.
Enthroned at 13 years old.
HE IS ONLY 21 YEARS OLD...
...BUT HIS RESPONSIBILITIES ARE SO GREAT...
I'M SORRY TO HAVE DISTURBED YOU AT NIGHT.
PLEASE CONTINUE WITH YOUR DUTIES.
TCH! THEY FINALLY CAME OUT!
HURRY UP AND LEAVE!!

EX-CUSE ME! I WOULD LIKE TO CHECK ON OUR LORD.
THERE IS PROBABLY NO GREATER POISON THAN STRESS FOR A SICK PATIENT...
...SO IT WAS LIKE IEMOCHI WAS BEING POISONED EVERY DAY.
NO! HIS PULSE IS RACING!
HE'S BREATH-ING FAST TOO. IT IS A CLEAR SIGN OF HEART FAILURE.
HAHH HAHH
DAMN IT!!
I AM NOT GOING TO LET HIM DIE HERE!!

*A medicine created from the poisonous secretions of dried blister beetles.

"Spring" and "Plum" allude to the names "Oharu" (which contains the kanji for spring) and "Umetaro" (Sakamoto Ryoma's alias, which contains the kanji for plum). —Ed.

WE, THE WESTERN MEDICINE DOCTORS, AGREE WITH MATSUMOTO HOGEN'S SUGGES-TION.
WE WOULD LIKE THE ELDERS' PERMIS-SION TO IMPLEMENT IT.
WE, THE CHINESE MEDICINE DOCTORS, STRONGLY REJECT IT!
PLEASE CONSIDER THIS CARE-FULLY!
HMM ...
IF THE "TRUE PATH" MEMBERS DISAGREE, THEN I GUESS THERE IS NO CHOICE. RIGHT, IGANOKAMI-DONO?
PUTTING THE SHOGUN'S LIFE IN DANGER IS OUT OF THE QUESTION!!
YOU STILL WON'T CHANGE YOUR MIND?!
IN THAT CASE!
IKINO-KAMI-SAMA!

*Back then, April–June were the calendar's summer months.

THERE IS ALWAYS AN INCREASE IN BERIBERI PATIENTS IN THE SUMMER...
...AND IT IS ALSO SUMMER WHEN THEIR CONDITIONS RAPIDLY DECLINE.
HOW IS LORD IEMOCHI DOING...?
AH
THINKING ABOUT IT WON'T DO ANYTHING!!
SWP SWP
I SHOULD BE TRAINING FOR RETURNING TO THE FIRST TROOP RATHER THAN SPENDING TIME BEING WORRIED ABOUT THIS!!
BAM!!
!!
ARE YOU STUPID, KAMIYA?
I'M SORRYY ...
I CAN SEE STARS FLYING ABOVE ME...
YOU'VE GOT A NOSE-BLEED!
TCH, WHAT A PAIN IN THE NECK.

LIE DOWN FOR A WHILE!
EEEEEEEK!
WHAT ARE YOU DOING, VICE CAPTAIN HIJIKATA!!
WHAT DO YOU MEAN?
THIS BEHAVIOR IS NOT LIKE YOU!
IT MIGHT TRIGGER SOME SORT OF MISFOR-TUNE!!
IT'S NOT LIKE ME TO DO SOMETHING LIKE THIS? HOW RUDE!!
I'VE ALWAYS BEEN KIND TO WOMEN, SINCE WAY BACK, AND...
!!
SHOCK
OH...

MY TONGUE SLIPPED.
I'M SORRY, KAMIYA!
I'LL... GO AND WASH MY FACE!
DMP
IT'S ALL RIGHT.
HE HASN'T FOUND OUT.
CALM DOWN, KAMIYA SEIZA-BURO.
EVEN IF HE KNOWS THAT I HAVE THE BODY OF A GIRL...
...HE STILL BELIEVES IT IS BECAUSE OF AN ILLNESS.
...
I SERI-OUSLY...
...NEED TO DO SOME-THING ABOUT THIS...

HIJI-KATA-SAN...
...HAS NOTICED?
BUT IT DOESN'T SEEM LIKE HE HAS DOUBTS ABOUT FEMININ-TITIS.
IS IT NATURAL INTUITION?
DOES HE KNOW BY INSTINCT?
HE SEEMS TO BE GRADUALLY REALIZING THAT KAMIYA-SAN IS A GIRL.
IF HE FINDS OUT THAT SHE IS A GIRL...
...HIJI-KATA-SAN WILL...
SOJI?

WHAT ARE YOU DOING?
HUPP
OH, NO ...!!
I-I DID COME HERE FOR SOME-THING ...
...BUT I'VE FOR-GOTTEN WHAT IT WAS...
...SO I'LL COME BACK LATER!
...
BAM!
TCH. I CAN'T BEAR TO WITNESS THEIR TEDIOUS METHODS!!
MATSU-MOTO HOGEN.
RESTRAIN YOUR-SELF.
YOU ARE INSIDE THE SHOGUN'S CASTLE.
WELL, I'M SORRY FOR SEEMING ILL-BRED!!

THE MAIN ILLNESS MAY BE BERI-BERI...
...BUT THE MAIN CAUSE OF THE SHOGUN'S PAIN RIGHT NOW IS THE EDEMA!
WE HAVE TO DEAL WITH THAT AS SOON AS POSSIBLE OR HE MAY JUST ABANDON HIS WILL TO LIVE!
HOW MUCH TIME ARE THOSE GEEZERS GOING TO WASTE?!
BERI-BERI?
BUT ISN'T THE ILLNESS RHEUMA-TISM?
AT THIS POINT, I BELIEVE THE MOST PLAUSIBLE DIAGNOSIS IS HEART FAILURE CAUSED BY BERIBERI.
ARE YOU CLAIMING THAT IT IS BERIBERI JUST AS THOSE CHINESE MEDICINE DOCTORS SAID?!
I WOULDN'T RULE OUT THE POSSIBILITY OF RHEUMA-TISM...
...BUT JUDGING FROM THE PROGRESS OF THE ILLNESS...
ARE YOU SAYING TAKENOUCHI HOIN'S DIAGNOSIS IS WRONG?!
AAARGH, STOP THIS! WHO CARES WHAT IT IS?!
OSAJI-SAMA!

!!
THE SHOGUN ...!!
GAH GEH GAH
MY LORD!!
HOW LONG HAS HE BEEN LIKE THIS?!
S-SINCE YESTERDAY... HE HAS GOTTEN NAUSEOUS EVERY TIME HE EATS, AND HASN'T EVEN BEEN ABLE TO HAVE HIS FAVORITE SWEETS.
HE VOMITED SEVERELY THIS TIME...
...AND HAS HARDLY URINATED IN THE LAST TWO DAYS...
HE HAS DEVELOPED EDEMA IN HIS FACE TOO!
HAA HAA

ELDERS!
I WILL TAKE RESPONSIBILITY IF ANYTHING HAPPENS...
SO PLEASE GRANT ME PERMISSION TO USE THE CANTHARIDIN BLISTERING OINTMENT!!
U-UMM... WELL...
FINE.
DO AS YOU LIKE, MATSUMOTO.
MY LORD?!
YOU SAID YOU WILL STAKE YOUR LIFE...
HAA
HAA
THEN I TOO MUST STAKE MY LIFE...OR I WILL LOSE MY HONOR AS A BUSHI, RIGHT?

THANK YOU VERY MUCH!!
BRING A PAIL OF HOT WATER!
WE NEED TO CLEAN HIS BODY FIRST!
AFTER THAT WE WILL APPLY THE OINTMENT OVER HIS HEART...
...AND USE A DIURETIC OF NEU-TRALIZED SALT...

SHU...
PHEW
HE...HAS FINALLY FALLEN ASLEEP...
POIK
SHOCK
!?
I WANT TO GO TO THE TOILET...
AAAH ...!!
AFTER THIS DAY...

...IEMOCHI BEGAN TO URINATE AGAIN...
...AND THE EDEMA GRADUALLY BEGAN TO RESOLVE.
IN SOME WAYS, IT WAS THE MOMENT THAT WESTERN MEDICINE PREVAILED OVER CHINESE MEDICINE.
RYOJUN...
YES SIR!
YOU ARE A COMRADE WHO STAKED YOUR LIFE ON ME...
FROM NOW ON, YOU MUST NEVER LEAVE MY SIDE.
IS THAT UNDERSTOOD?
IT IS AN HONOR...
...TO HEAR SUCH WELCOME WORDS FROM YOU!!
USUALLY, THE PRIVATE DOCTORS WOULD HAVE SWITCHED OUT WITH ONE ANOTHER AFTER TWO HOURS WITH THE SHOGUN...
...BUT RYOJUN RECEIVED THIS SPECIAL ORDER TO STAY BY HIS SIDE ALL DAY.

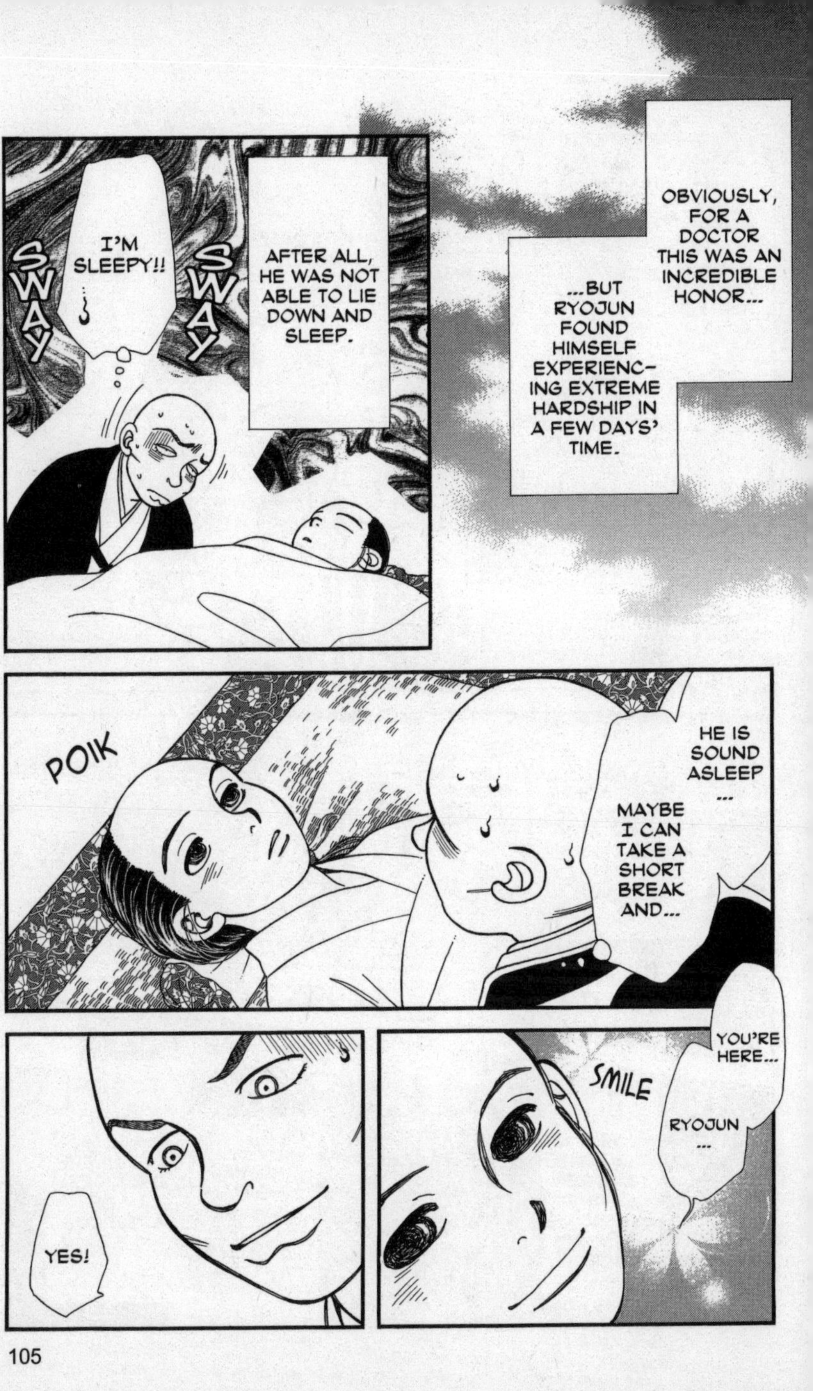
OBVIOUSLY, FOR A DOCTOR THIS WAS AN INCREDIBLE HONOR...
...BUT RYOJUN FOUND HIMSELF EXPERIENCING EXTREME HARDSHIP IN A FEW DAYS' TIME.
AFTER ALL, HE WAS NOT ABLE TO LIE DOWN AND SLEEP.
SWAY
I'M SLEEPY!! ...
SWAY
HE IS SOUND ASLEEP...
MAYBE I CAN TAKE A SHORT BREAK AND...
POIK
YOU'RE HERE...
RYOJUN...
SMILE
YES!

HE'S CUTE!
HE'S SO CUTE!!
SNORE
HOW CAN I BETRAY HIM?!
IEMOCHI GREW FOND OF RYOJUN AS IF HE WERE A SMALL CHILD.
HE WAS ENTHRONED AT 13 YEARS OLD...
...HE MUST HAVE NEVER HAD A FAMILY MEMBER WHO HE COULD DEPEND ON.
THE RETAINERS SYMPATHIZED WITH THE SHOGUN...
MY LORD.
WE HAVE RECEIVED A GIFT OF RED BEAN JELLY FOR YOU.
WE ALSO HAVE RED BEAN-FILLED WAFERS, TOO.
...AND DEDICATED THEMSELVES TO HIM WITH HOPES THAT HE WOULD FULLY RECOVER.
UNFORTUNATELY...
...THE SWEETS, WHICH WERE CONSIDERED TO BE NUTRITIOUS...
...WERE THE MAIN CAUSE OF THE VITAMIN B1 DEFICIENCY...
...WHICH WAS THE CAUSE OF THE SYMPTOMS OF BERIBERI.

THE EDEMA HAS BEGUN TO SWELL AGAIN.
HE IS FEELING GENERAL FATIGUE ...
...AND HIS HEARTBEAT HAS BECOME INCREASINGLY IRREGULAR.
THE TREATMENT I PROVIDED HIM HAS REACHED ITS LIMIT.
BUT WHAT ELSE CAN I DO...?
...!!
AH
RYOJUN...
YOU WERE DOZING OFF AGAIN...
PLEASE FORGIVE ME.
HOWEVER, IT HAS BEEN ABOUT 20 DAYS THAT I HAVE REMAINED BY YOUR SIDE, MY LORD.
WOULD IT BE POSSIBLE FOR ME TO TAKE A TWO-HOUR REST?
I SEE...
I AM SORRY THAT YOU HAVE NOT HAD ANY REST FOR 20 DAYS...

AND?!
BUT I AM AFRAID OF PARTING WITH YOU FOR EVEN A SHORT WHILE.
AH ...
DROOP
BUT DO I WANT YOU TO GET SOME REST...
...SO I WILL SCOOT OVER TO ONE SIDE OF MY FUTON ...
YOU MAY SLEEP WITH ME HERE.
SLEEP WITH THE SHOGUN?!
TH-THAT IS OUT OF THE QUESTION !!
SOME-ONE.
BRING ME ANOTHER PILLOW.
YES, MY LORD!
DON'T YOU WANT TO USE MY FUTON?

ACK...
He's staring at me like a three-year-old...
EXCUSE ME...
THERE IS NO NEED TO BE SO MODEST.
TAKE YOUR TIME AND SLEEP AS MUCH AS YOU WANT...
HOW COULD I SLEEP?!
POIK POIK
...
Why is this happening?
MIYA SENT ME ANOTHER LETTER...
I WILL TELL HER ABOUT THIS IN-CIDENT...
...ONCE I HAVE RECOV-ERED ENOUGH TO WRITE BACK...
PLEASE DON'T.
I AM SURE MIYA WILL LAUGH AND HER CHEEKS WILL TURN BRIGHT RED...
LADY KAZUNO-MIYA IS SUCH A SWEET PERSON.

*Emperor Komei had sternly requested that Kazunomiya be treated as a member of the imperial family, even after she had married down into the Tokugawa family.

BUT HE MUST HAVE CALLED HER THAT WHEN THEY WERE ALONE.
"CHIKAKO."
"WILL I BE ABLE TO SEE HER AGAIN?"
OF COURSE...
...MY LORD!
I SHALL LEAD YOU TO FULL RECOVERY...
...WITH MY LIFE AT STAKE...
AND IF THAT COMES TRUE...
...I AM WILLING TO GIVE MY LIFE TO HIM NO MATTER HOW MANY TIMES I AM REBORN!!
HOWEVER...
...THIS PROMISE WOULD NEVER BE FULFILLED.

MY LORD!
MY LORD.
MY LORD.
MY LORD ...
...

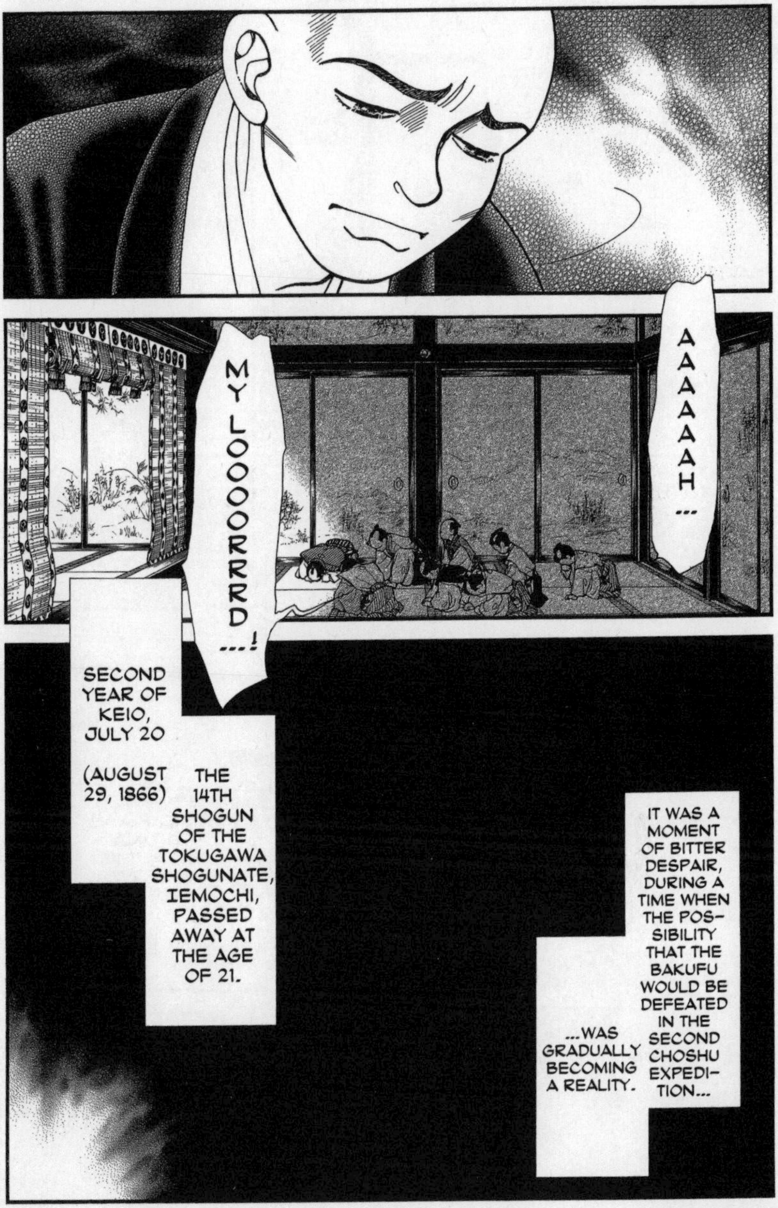
AAAAAAH...
MY LOOOORRRD...!
SECOND YEAR OF KEIO, JULY 20
(AUGUST 29, 1866)
THE 14TH SHOGUN OF THE TOKUGAWA SHOGUNATE, IEMOCHI, PASSED AWAY AT THE AGE OF 21.
IT WAS A MOMENT OF BITTER DESPAIR, DURING A TIME WHEN THE POS-SIBILITY THAT THE BAKUFU WOULD BE DEFEATED IN THE SECOND CHOSHU EXPEDI-TION...
...WAS GRADUALLY BECOMING A REALITY.

WHAT ...?!
NO...
IT CAN'T BE!
IT'S POINTLESS TO CRY OVER IT.
THE OFFICIAL ANNOUNCEMENT WILL BE MADE ON AUGUST 20.
THE BAKUFU STILL HAS...
...A LOT OF WORK TO DO BEFORE THEN IN ORDER TO KEEP ANY TURMOIL TO A MINIMUM.
OF COURSE, THIS WILL BE KEPT TOP SECRET WHILE WE CARRY OUT OUR DUTIES HERE, TOO.
THE ASSISTANT VICE CAPTAINS MAY ONLY REVEAL THIS NEWS TO THEIR GOCHO.
UNDER-STOOD!
KAMIYA!
IF YOU'VE GOT NOTHING ELSE TO DO BUT CRY, GET OUT!
N...
NO!!
I'M SORRY!

HIJIKATA-SAN SURE IS STRICT.
AND KAMIYA-SAN HAS LEARNED TO HOLD BACK HER TEARS, TOO.
working as a clerk today
SHE KEPT COMPLAINING ABOUT HOW SHE HATED THIS...
...BUT SHE'S USED HER DISSATISFACTION TO IMPROVE HERSELF.
THIS IS...
...PROBABLY WHERE YOU ARE MEANT TO BE.
WE TRAVELED TO FUSHIMI TOGETHER IN PURSUIT OF THE SHOGUN.
WHEN WAS THAT AGAIN?

THIS PLACE BRINGS BACK MEMORIES TOO.
"THE CRY-BABY TREE."
KAMIYA-SAN...
...WOULD COME HERE TO CRY ALL THE TIME.
I HAVE A FEELING...
...THAT THOSE MEMORIES WILL VANISH LIKE SOAP BUBBLES, ALONG WITH LORD IEMOCHI'S LIFE...
THE SUNSET IS BEAUTIFUL...

SATISFIED NOW, SOJI?
SHE HAS A NEW PLACE TO CRY NOW.
AND IT'S WITH THE BEST PERSON...
...THAT YOU YOURSELF COULD HAVE HOPED FOR...

WHAAAAT?!
WHAT ARE YOU DOING HERE, OKITA SENSEI?!
...!!
DID YOU COME HERE TO WIPE AWAY MY TEARS AGAIN?
CLIMB CLIMB CLIMB
JUST KIDDING.
Ha ha.
WHY ARE YOU LOOKING AT ME LIKE THAT?
B- BUT ...

WHAT ABOUT HIJIKATA-SAN?
I PREPARED HIS DINNER AND ASKED TO HAVE SOME TIME OFF.
HE PROBABLY KNEW THAT I WAS GOING TO COME HERE AND CRY.
BUT I'VE KEPT IT A SECRET FOR NEARLY TWO MONTHS NOW, WITHOUT TELLING ANYBODY...
SO I CAN CRY A LITTLE, CAN'T I?
I DON'T THINK IT'S A "LITTLE" ANYMORE.
WAH...
WAAAAARGH!
WAAAARGH!
WAH...

OKITA SENSEI ...?
YOU MUSTN'T ...
IT'S STILL SUPPOSED TO BE A SECRET.
OH, RIGHT!
slow, as usual.
AS EXPECTED...
...THE BAKUFU'S SECRET EVENTUALLY THREW EVERYTHING INTO CHAOS.

KAZE HIKARU
SENRYU
By Miki Minagawa-san from Chiba
EVERY TIME
HER FEMININITY GROWS
SO DO HER EYELASHES

KAZE HIKARU SENRYU

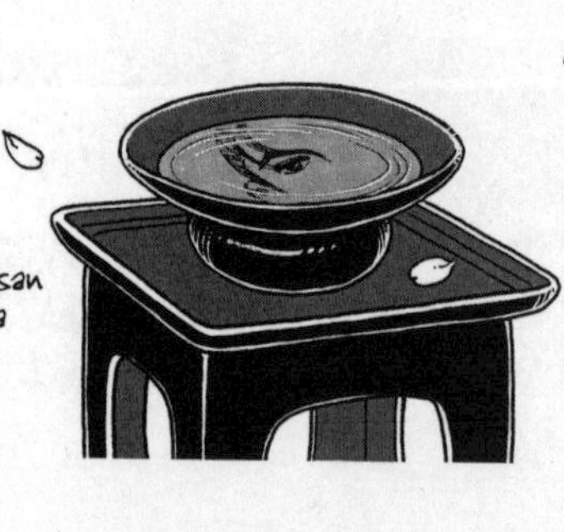

By satsukibare-san from Osaka

THE TEARS OF THE ONI'S EYES GENTLY TURN TO SAKE

IT'S NOT THAT BIG OF A SURPRISE, IS IT?
THAT GUY'S BEEN AFTER THAT SEAT FOR AGES.
HE'D NEVER MISS OUT ON A GREAT OPPORTUNITY LIKE THIS.
DON'T SAY SUCH THINGS, TOSHI!
IEMOCHI-SAMA PASSED AWAY VERY RECENTLY...
...SO HITO-TSUBASHI-KO MUST ALSO BE FILLED WITH SORROW!!
ON TOP OF THAT, THE CHOSHU EXPEDITION IS CLEARLY HEADED TOWARD DEFEAT, AND YOU'RE CALLING THIS A "GREAT OPPORTU-NITY"?!
THE TOKUGAWA BAKUFU MAY COME TO AN END, YOU KNOW?!
AH...
You're so embarrassing..
OKAY, I'M SORRY. STOP CRYING.
NO...

IT DEPENDS ON HOW YOU LOOK AT IT, CAPTAIN.
THE SHOGUN'S DEATH WAS UNDOUBT-EDLY A MIS-FORTUNE ...
...BUT IT MAY TURN OUT TO BE A RAY OF LIGHT FOR THE BAKUFU.
WHAT DO YOU MEAN BY THAT, COUNCILOR ITO?!
TOP THREE MEETING
...
KAMIYA ...
I'M SORRY.
YOU WANT ME TO LEAVE, DON'T YOU?
DON'T COME BACK UNTIL 4 P.M.!
I DID IT AGAIN...

I WOULDN'T HAVE GOTTEN KICKED OUT IF I PRETENDED NOT TO HEAR THEM...
BUT IT MAY TURN OUT TO BE SOMETHING THAT WILL UNNERVE ME AGAIN IF I DO HEAR IT...
THE POSSIBILITY OF HITOTSU-BASHI-KO BECOMING THE NEXT SHOGUN IS SHOCKING ENOUGH FOR ME...
GONG
OWW!!
KAMIYA-SAN?!
WHY WEREN'T YOU PAYING ATTENTION AGAIN?
WHAT?!
OH, O-OKITA SENSEI.
AH.
SORRY ABOUT YESTER-DAY.
I WAS A BOTHER TO YOU AGAIN...
It made me very happy, though.

Replay
I'M USED TO YOUR TEARS, KAMIYA-SAN.
WHAT?
OH, THAT WAS NOTHING...
WHAT?!
THEN YOU REALLY DID COME FOR ME?!
UM... EH, WELL...
WHERE DID YOU AMBUSH KAMIYA, OKITA-SAN?
S-SAITO-SAN!
YOU'RE MAKING A MISTAKE, SAITO SENSEI.
OKITA SENSEI WAS KIND, AND...

HOW LEISURELY OF YOU...
...TO HAVE BEEN ENJOYING A TRYST WHEN THE BAKUFU IS BUSILY TRYING TO CHOOSE THE NEXT SHOGUN.
HOW DO YOU KNOW THAT?!
IT'S JUST A HUNCH!
AMAZING.
I THOUGHT YOU WERE FOLLOWING ME AROUND!
I'D NEVER FOLLOW YOU!!
I'd follow Kamiya!!
BA-BUMP
BA-BUMP
THEN...
...WHO DO YOU THINK WILL BE THE NEXT SHOGUN...
...ACCORDING TO THAT HUNCH OF YOURS, SAITO SENSEI?
HITOTSUBASHI YOSHINOBU-KO, WITH NO DOUBT.

OH, UKINO-SUKE-SAN?!
UKINO-SUKE?
H-HOW CAN YOU BE SO SURE?!
AREN'T THERE OTHER CANDI-DATES?
THERE ARE, BUT KAMENO-SUKE-SAMA OF THE TAYASU FAMILY IS STILL FOUR YEARS OLD.
MOCHI-TSUGU-SAMA OF THE KISHU FAMILY IS 23, BUT HE IS SAID TO BE THE EPITOME OF MEDI-OCRITY.
IT WOULD ONLY BE A BURDEN FOR HIM TO BECOME THE SHOGUN AT A RISKY MOMENT LIKE THIS.
ON THE OTHER HAND, HITOTSUBASHI-KO IS 30, AND IN THE PRIME OF HIS LIFE. HE IS FAMOUS FOR BEING BOLD AND BRILLIANT. AND HE IS FROM A RIGHTEOUS FAMILY TOO.
WHAT REASON IS THERE *NOT* TO CHOOSE HIM AS THE HEIR?
BUT HE IS AN AWFUL PERSON!!
I'VE HEARD THAT, TOO.
HOWEVER, THOSE WHO ARE EXCEEDINGLY SMART TEND TO RECEIVE SUCH CRITICISM.

THE TOKUGAWA BAKUFU IS FACING THE GREATEST THREAT IT HAS EVER EXPERIENCED SINCE ITS BIRTH.
EVEN THOUGH HE MAY BE A DIFFICULT PERSON, I BELIEVE THERE IS NO ONE BETTER THAN HITOTSUBASHI-KO TO ADDRESS THIS SITUATION.
ARE YOU UNHAPPY ABOUT IT, KAMIYA?
N-NO!
I DO NOT DISAGREE, IF THAT IS YOUR OPINION, BUT...
WELL... I'M A LITTLE WORRIED...
HE WAS AN INTERESTING MAN.
I SEE.
YOU TWO HAVE MET HIM BEFORE, HAVEN'T YOU?
Am I jealous?
THAT MAN, WHO POSES AS "UKINOSUKE," THE PRODIGAL SON OF A RICH MERCHANT...
...WILL BE THE 15TH SHOGUN OF TOKUGAWA?

MEAN-WHILE, AT OSAKA CASTLE ...
I...
...REFUSE, UNCONDITIONALLY!!
HITO-TSU-BASHI-DONO!
NEVER!!
I WILL NOT BECOME SHOGUN!!
B-BUT...
...ALTHOUGH YOU CONCEDED TO IEMOCHI-SAMA, YOU ALSO HAD EVERY RIGHT TO BECOME THE 14TH SHOGUN.
WHY ARE YOU REJECTING THE OFFER NOW?
THAT IS EXACTLY WHY!

NEVER IN MY LIFE HAVE I PERSONALLY WANTED TO BECOME THE SHOGUN!
THE REASON I FOUGHT OVER THE SEAT OF THE 14TH SHOGUN WASN'T BECAUSE I WANTED TO, BUT BECAUSE MY FATHER AND THE OTHERS SET ME UP TO IT!
HAVE YOU ANY IDEA THE BITTERNESS OF THAT EXPERI-ENCE?!
THE MERE THOUGHT OF IT DISGUSTS ME!
IF I BECAME THE SHOGUN NOW, PEOPLE WOULD THINK THAT I WAS HOPING TO BECOME THE SHOGUN ALL ALONG.
BUT I WILL NEVER ACCEPT THAT!!
I WOULD RATHER DIE THAN BECOME THE SHOGUN!!
BAM!
HITO-TSU-BASHI-DONO!

DMP DMP DMP DMP DM
HITOTSUBASHIKO... ...WHERE ARE YOU GOING?!
HITOTSUBASHIKO?!
HITOTSUBASHIDONO...!
SHYOOOO...

DAMN YOU!
WHY DID YOU HAVE TO DIE BEFORE ME, IEMOCHI?!
YOU'RE THE ONE WHO KILLED MY PRIDE FIRST!
HOW DARE YOU YOURSELF DIE!
HITOTSUBASHI-DONO...

JUST KID-DING... ♡
HUUUH?!
...?!
HEY, HIGO. YOU'RE HERE, TOO?
TAKE CARE OF THE REST FOR ME.
H-HITO-TSUBA...
FARE-WELL!
HITO-TSU-BASHI-DONO-OO?!
THE OUTCOME OF THE CHOSHU EXPEDITION IS ALREADY CLEAR.

IF THE WAR CONTINUES, THE BAKUFU ARMY IS SURE TO LOSE...
...AND THAT IN TURN WILL PROVE TO THE NATION THAT THE TOKUGAWA BAKUFU HAS COLLAPSED.
ITO-SAN, MUST YOU BE SO HARSH?!
WELL THEN, HIJIKATA-KUN...
DO YOU THINK THERE IS ANY CHANCE THAT THE BAKUFU CAN WIN THIS WAR?
I HATE TO AGREE WITH YOU, BUT...
WITH THE CURRENT STATE OF THE BAKUFU ARMY...
NO.
TOSHI!
IN THAT CASE...
THE ONLY REMAINING PATH FOR THE TOKUGAWA BAKUFU IS TO BRING THIS WAR TO A CEASEFIRE.
HOWEVER, TO MAKE THAT PROPOSAL IS NO DIFFERENT FROM DECLARING DEFEAT.
IT WOULD BE A BREACH OF FAITH AGAINST EMPEROR KOMEI, WHO GAVE THE IMPERIAL ORDER FOR THE EXPEDITION.
BUT THAT IS WHERE IEMOCHI-SAMA COMES IN!

*Hitotsubashi Yoshinobu's nickname.

ONCE A BUSHI BEGINS IN BATTLE, THEY DON'T LOSE FACE IN DEFEAT, BUT LOSE THEIR LIVES INSTEAD!
IF THE BAKUFU IS JUST A BUNCH OF GUTLESS LOSERS...
...THEN IT'S JUST AS WELL THAT THEY COLLAPSE!
THAT IS ENOUGH, HIJIKATA TOSHIZO!!
NO MATTER HOW CORRUPT THOSE SO-CALLED LOYAL RETAINERS ARE...
...WE VOWED TO PROTECT THE TOKUGAWA FAMILY UNTIL THE END, AS TRUE BUSHI!!
IS THAT NOT WHY WE ROSE UP?!

RIGHT...
YOU'RE RIGHT.
KONDO-SAN.
SORRY.
I WAS BEING TOO PESSIMISTIC.
I UNDERSTAND.
YOU SAID THAT BECAUSE YOU CARE ABOUT THE TOKUGAWA.
YOU HID YOUR TRUE FEELINGS WELL, HIJIKATA-KUN.
BUT JUST NOW I SAW THROUGH YOU FOR A MOMENT.
YOUR FEELINGS HAVE ALREADY PARTED WAYS WITH THE TOKUGAWA.
BUT YOU HAVE NOT REALIZED...
...THAT IS THE SAME AS PARTING WAYS WITH KONDO.

I HAVE NO DOUBT...
...THAT YOU WILL COME TO MY SIDE SOONER OR LATER.
AND THAT IS WHEN THE TOKUGAWA WILL MEET ITS DEMISE!
THAT MAN HAS TO BE CRAZY...
WHO?
COUNCILOR ITO?
WHY THE HELL WOULD I BE TALKING ABOUT THE COUNCILOR NOW?!
I'M TALKING ABOUT UKINOSUKE-SAN, OF COURSE!
AREN'T YOU WORRIED?
THAT A PLEASURE-SEEKING, IRRESPONSIBLE, CONDESCENDING CYNIC LIKE HIM...
EH, KAMIYA-SAN.
WHY ARE YOU PARTICIPATING IN THE ROUNDS WITH THE FIRST TROOP AGAIN?

THE VICE CAPTAIN TOLD ME NOT TO RETURN UNTIL 4 P.M....
THEN WHY DON'T YOU GET SOME REST FOR A CHANGE?
AM I BEING A NUISANCE?
NO... YOU'RE NOT BEING A NUISANCE, BUT...
But I feel uneasy.
WOULD YOU PLEASE PERMIT ME TO JOIN YOU JUST FOR TODAY?
Oh? Is he in a bad mood?
What?
YOU'RE THE ONLY PERSON I CAN SPEAK WITH ABOUT UKINO-SUKE-SAN, OKITA SENSEI.
I AM AWARE THAT I LACK TRAINING, BUT...BUT I...
I FEEL LIKE I AM GOING TO EXPLODE...
...IF I DON'T LET OUT THE CONFUSED THOUGHTS INSIDE OF ME!!
I-I WOULD NOT WANT TO SEE THAT HAPPEN...

I WILL NOT INTERFERE WITH YOUR WORK.
YOU JUST NEED TO PRETEND TO LISTEN.
I WILL FEEL A LITTLE MORE COMFORT-ABLE...
...IF YOU KEEP SMILING, SENSEI.
YOU...
...MAKE IT SOUND LIKE I'M A JIZO STATUE...
I'LL MAKE AN OFFER-ING OF SWEETS LATER ON!
HA HA HA, I HATE MYSELF.
OKITA JIZO WILL BE EASILY SWAYED BY SIMPLE PLEASURES LIKE THAT...

!!
...
COULD IT BE ...?!
SODA-SAN!
TAKE CARE OF THE REST OF THE ROUND FOR ME.
I WILL EXPLAIN EVERYTHING AT HEADQUARTERS!
R-ROGER!

IMPOS-SIBLE.
BUT THAT WAS...
UKINO-SUKE-SAN?!
YOOOOOOO!!
OKITA SOJI AND KAMIYA SEIZABURO!
LONG TIME NO SEE, YOU TWO!

HE'S DEAD DRUNK?!
OKITA... AS IN...
SHIN-SEN-GUMI?!
EEEEEEK!
UKI-SAMA! YOU HAVE TO BOW DOWN!
HUUUH?!
HUUUH?!
WE'LL BE BEHEADED IF WE DON'T APOLOGIZE!!
IS THERE A ROOM NEARBY WHERE WE CAN BE ALONE?
OH NO, IT'S FINE!
UKINOSUKE-SAN!
WHERE IS OYOSHI-SAN AND MATSUZO-SAN?!
HAA HA HA HA!
I THREW THEM OFF MY TRACKS!!
THEY WERE BEING ANNOYING, SO...
I DON'T WANT TO BELIEVE...
SEIZABURO. ♡ I WANTED TO SEE YOU SO MUCH. ♡
...THAT THIS DRUNKARD WILL BE THE NEXT SHOGUN!!

PLEASE LET HIM OFF THE HOOK...
...HITOTSUBASHIKO.
YOU ARE NOT AS DRUNK AS YOU SEEM, I PRESUME.
WHAT?!
TCH.
YOU REALLY ARE IMPOSSIBLE TO DECEIVE, OKITA SOJI.
I'M DRINKING LIKE A FISH...
...BUT I CAN'T GET DRUNK. SO WHAT AM I SUPPOSED TO DO?!
BUT...
TH-THIS IS NOT THE TIME OR PLACE FOR YOU TO BE FOOLING AROUND!!
Y-YOU'RE SUPPOSED TO SUCCEED THE SHOGUN!
AH, I TURNED IT DOWN.

HUUH?!
YOU TURNED DOWN THE JOB OF SHOGUN?!
THE CHANCE TO BECOME THE GREATEST LORD OF THIS NATION?!
I THOUGHT YOU DESIRED THAT POSITION ALL THIS TIME!
AHHH, THAT'S EXACTLY IT!!
I HATE HOW EVERYONE THINKS THAT!
I AM NOT SUITED FOR THAT JOB!!
I'VE GOT NO INTENTION OF DOING IT!
YOU...
...ARE QUITE AWARE OF WHAT KIND OF PERSON YOU ARE, UKINO SUKE-SAN.
I KNOW. DO YOU LOVE ME NOW?
YET...
...THERE ARE MANY PEOPLE IN THE BAKUFU WHO THINK THAT NO ONE IS MORE SUITED THAN YOU.
I BELIEVE YOU ARE IN NO POSITION TO FOLLOW YOUR WHIMS UNTIL ANOTHER SUCCESSOR HAS BEEN CHOSEN.
I DON'T LIKE YOU.
LEAVE.

WE'RE LEAVING.
BUT ONLY AFTER WE HAVE TAKEN YOU BACK.
I'M NOT GOING.
I'M GOING TO PLAY WITH SEIZABURO HERE. ♡
NO WAY!!
c'mon, let's go home.
YOU'RE PLAYING HARD TO GET, AS ALWAYS.
DOES MAKING LOVE WITH OKITA FEEL THAT GOOD?
BAM BAM BAM
THAT IS NONE OF YOUR BUSINESS!!
STOP SULKING AND HURRY BACK HOME! EVERYONE'S WORRIED ABOUT YOU!!
THIS IS ANNOYING. HOW COME YOU TWO ARE BEING SO BASHFUL?
AND DO YOU REALIZE YOUR HEADS ARE TOO HIGH?
YES SIIIIIR!!
HA HA HA.
SOCIAL STATUS IS SO RIDICULOUS!

YOU GUYS...
ARE YOU GOING TO PROTECT THE TOKUGAWA BAKUFU WITH YOUR LIVES EVEN AFTER I BECOME THE SHOGUN?
ACK ...!!
OF COURSE.
HA.
YOU'RE A LIAR, OKITA.
YOU SHOULD LEARN FROM SEIZA-BURO'S HONESTY.
YOU DO NOT NEED TO BELIEVE ME.
BUT WHOMEVER THE SHOGUN IS, MY LORD WILL ALWAYS BE NONE OTHER THAN CAPTAIN KONDO ISAMI.
SO I WILL PROTECT THE TOKUGAWA BAKUFU AS LONG AS THE CAPTAIN DOES NOT TURN HIS BACK ON THEM.

HMM ...
THEN IF THE CAPTAIN SWITCHES SIDES TO CHOSHU, YOU'LL DO THE SAME?
OKITA SENSEI ...!
YES.
WHAT IF HE ORDERED YOU TO *DIE*?
I WOULD DIE, OF COURSE.
YOUR SHUDO PARTNER IS AN IDIOT, SEIZABURO!!
WITH ALL DUE RESPECT, HITOTSUBASHI-KO ...
IDIOCY IS A TRAIT OF ALL TRUE BUSHI.
EVEN IF THEIR SHOGUN TURNS OUT TO BE A BASTARD ...
...THEY WILL STAKE THEIR LIVES ON HIM ONCE THEIR MINDS ARE MADE UP.

I, SEIZABURO, HAVE BECOME COMMITTED JUST NOW!
BOW
OKITA SENSEI AND I WILL PROTECT YOU WITH OUR LIVES...
SO PLEASE RETURN TO YOUR MANOR...
MY LORD!
...!
VERY WELL ...
IF YOU MEAN THAT FROM THE BOTTOM OF YOUR HEART...
KAMIYA SEIZABURO.
I ORDER YOU TO SPEND THE NIGHT WITH ME TONIGHT.

WHAT?!
SPEND THE NIGHT?!
YOU KNOW. ♡
IF YOU MANAGE TO SATISFY ME WITHOUT RUNNING AWAY BEFORE DAWN...
...I PROMISE YOU THAT I WILL GO BACK.
THAT'S...
AND OKITA...
YOU MUST LEAVE.
WHAAT?! I REJECT THAT ORDER!!
SENSEI, YOU MUSTN'T BETRAY HIM THAT QUICKLY...
BUT, KAMIYA-SAN...!
IS THAT AN ORDER FROM THE SHOGUN?!
IF I SPEND THE NIGHT WITH YOU...
I WILL AGREE TO ACCEPT THE POSITION OF SHOGUN.
UH-HUH. OKAY.

KAZE HIKARU SENRYU

KAZE HIKARU
I GOT HOOKED ON IT
AND NOW I'M A BAKUMATSU MASTER

By Tao-san from Fukui

DO YOU KNOW WHAT SPENDING THE NIGHT WITH HIM *MEANS*?!
DO YOU THINK I DON'T, OKITA SENSEI!?
I'M 18 YEARS OLD, YOU KNOW?!
THEN ...
...YOU ARE...
...PRE-PARED TO GO SO FAR AS SLEEPING WITH HIM...?!
I DON'T WANT TO!!
BUT UNLESS UKINOSUKE-SAN AGREES, THE SHOGUN'S POSITION WILL REMAIN OPEN.
CONSIDER-ING HOW DANGEROUS THAT COULD BE FOR THE TOKUGAWA FAMILY...
...THIS IS NO TIME FOR THE LIKES OF ME TO BE COMPLAINING.

I WILL NOT REGRET OFFERING MYSELF FOR THIS MISSION.
I JUST NEED...
I AM...
...A BUSHI.
...TO RESIST RUNNING AWAY UNTIL THE MORNING!
K...
KAMIYA-SAN...!
PLEASE WIPE THAT EXPRESSION OFF YOUR FACE, OKITA SENSEI.
I'LL GET THROUGH IT SOME-HOW.
HOW?!
YOU ARE A GIRL!!

IT IS UNCONSCIONABLE FOR YOU TO BE MADE INTO A PLAYTHING LIKE THIS!
SHHH!!
HUSH, OKITA SENSEI!!
HOW LONG ARE YOU GOING TO KEEP CHATTING OUT THERE?!
BEAT IT, OKITA SOJI.
AND REMEMBER, IF YOU TALK TO ANYONE ABOUT THIS OR DECIDE TO RETURN...
...I WITHDRAW EVERYTHING I PROMISED.
...!
SENSEI.
PLEASE TRUST ME AND LEAVE THIS TO ME.
YOU NEED TO GO BACK TO HEADQUARTERS QUICKLY AND TELL THE VICE CAPTAIN THAT I AM UNABLE TO RETURN BECAUSE I HAVE SUDDENLY BECOME ILL OR SOMETHING...
OTHERWISE HE'LL PROBABLY ORDER ME TO COMMIT SEPPUKU WHEN I GET BACK TOMORROW.
PLEASE DO THAT FOR ME!
KAMIYA-SAN...!

"I AM A BUSHI."
IF I WERE IN KAMIYA-SAN'S POSITION...
...I WOULD PROBABLY MAKE THE SAME CHOICE.
KAMIYA-SAN IS TRYING TO FULFILL HER DUTY AS A BUSHI.
BUT I WANT TO STOP HER. BUT THAT IS ONLY...
...MY PERSONAL FEELING.

I MUST GO BACK TO HEAD-QUARTERS WITH A CALM MIND AND OBTAIN PERMISSION FOR KAMIYA-SAN TO STAY OUT FOR THE NIGHT.
I MUST FULFILL THE ONLY JOB I CAN DO AT THIS TIME, AS WELL.
FOR I, TOO, AM A BUSHI.
I CAN'T BELIEVE MY EYES...
HE REALLY DID LEAVE YOU.
BECAUSE THAT WAS YOUR ORDER, MY LORD.
WHY IS THAT A SUR-PRISE?

HUMPH.
BUSHI ARE SUCH...
...BORING CREATURES.
THEY WOULD WATCH THEIR LOVED ONE BEING SACRIFICED TO ANOTHER MAN...
...AND JUST BEAR IT IN ORDER TO DEMONSTRATE THEIR "LOYALTY."
Y...
BZZT
YOU'VE GOT NO RIGHT TO SAY THAT!!
BZZT
BZZT
NO, SEIZABURO!
I WILL BE PLAYING RIGHT INTO HIS HANDS IF I BECOME UPSET NOW!!
NO LOVE TRANSCENDS LOYALTY...
...IN THE WAY OF A BUSHI.
HMM.
I KNOW WHAT HE'S UP TO. THIS TWISTED MAN...
...JUST LOVES TO SEE PEOPLE PANICKING.
SO THE MOST IMPORTANT THING IS TO STAY CALM!

NOW, LET'S...
YES SIR!
I WILL PREPARE THE FUTON THIS MOMENT...
SWUP
CHA
EXCUSE ME!
IS ANYONE OUT HERE?!
EH, WHO NEEDS A... futon..
I SEE.
HE'S TRYING TO BUY TIME.
FINE.
THERE'S STILL A LOT OF TIME UNTIL THE MORNING.
I QUITE ENJOY IT WHEN THEY PLAY HARD TO GET.
IT LOOKS LIKE I'VE GOTTEN HOLD OF A FUN TOY.
AND SO...

*A moniker for any menstrual symptoms/disorders.

BA-BUMP
ARE YOU...
...REEE-AALLY NOT IN LOVE WITH KAMIYA?
WHAT...
B-BUT...
HE'S A MAN!
I DO NOT HAVE A TASTE FOR SHUDO.
RIGHT!!
I KNOW THAT!
I KNOW THAT, BUT...
...TO TELL YOU THE TRUTH, RECENTLY...
...I'VE HAD THE FEELING THAT MAYBE KAMIYA IS REALLY A GIRL...
I'M SERIOUS.
AND I CONSIDER MYSELF AN EXPERT ON WOMEN, TOO.

SO IN THAT CASE, HE WOULD BE THE PERFECT CHOICE FOR YOU, BECAUSE YOU DON'T GET ALONG WITH WOMEN!
I AM WORRIED THAT SOMETHING MIGHT HAPPEN IF YOU ACCIDENTALLY DID SOMETHING WITH HIM...
YOU ARE ...
...WORRIED ABOUT SOMETHING LIKE THAT, HIJIKATA-SAN?!
"SOMETHING LIKE THAT"?!
IF YOU EVER START TAKING AN INTEREST IN SHUDO, I'M SERIOUSLY GOING TO CUT TIES WITH YOU!!
I THINK *YOU* HAVE A HIGHER POSSIBILITY OF ACCIDENTALLY TAKING YOUR CHANCES ON HIM, HIJIKATA-SAN.
STOP IT!!
UNLIKE YOU, I'VE ALWAYS HAD MORE THAN ENOUGH WOMEN ON MY HANDS!
I'D NEVER FALL FOR A BRAT LIKE THAT!!
"BRAT" ...HUH.
THAT'S SUCH AN AWFUL THING TO SAY.

I'VE HAD ENOUGH OF YOUR REPORT!
IF SHE ISN'T A BRAT ANYMORE ...
LEAVE!
...MAYBE HIJIKATA-SAN CAN ...
...REC-OGNIZE THAT TOO.
KAMIYA-SAN...
I WONDER WHAT SHE'S DOING NOW.
DON'T THINK ABOUT IT.
ALONE WITH UKINO-SUKE-SAN...
DON'T THINK ABOUT IT, SOJI.
KAMIYA-SAN TOLD ME TO LEAVE IT TO HER.
I HOPE SHE ISN'T BEING FORCED TO DO SOMETHING SHE DOESN'T WANT.
DON'T THINK ABOUT IT.
EVEN IF I THINK ABOUT IT, THERE'S NOTHING I CAN DO.
YOU ARE USELESS.
...JI!

SOJI!
WHAT'S WRONG?!
AH...
EWWW...
I WAS IMAGINING SOMETHING SICK BECAUSE OF YOU, HIJIKATA-SAN...
LIKE WHAT?!
"IF YOU TALK TO ANYONE ABOUT THIS OR DECIDE TO RETURN...I WITHDRAW EVERYTHING I PROMISED."
I CAN'T DO ANYTHING.
BUT...
...IS THIS REALLY WHAT YOU WANT, SOJI?
AH, SODA-SAN.
THANK YOU VERY MUCH FOR TAKING CARE OF THE ROUNDS.
OH, NO PROBLEM.
DO YOU HAVE A SPECIAL MISSION TO ATTEND TO?
YES...
PRETEND TO BE CALM...
REMAIN SILENT AND UNMOVED...

ARE YOU JUST GOING TO...
...ENDURE THIS NIGHT WITHOUT SLEEPING?
WHAT WOULD SAITO-SAN DO...?
THAT'S RIGHT. KAMIYA-SAN IS IN TROUBLE.
HE WOULD HAVE SOME IDEAS!
AM I GOING TO TELL SOMEONE ELSE ABOUT THIS?
WHAT IF HITOTSUBASHI-KO FINDS OUT?
BUT...
ASSISTANT VICE CAPTAIN SAITO?
HE WENT OUT FOR A DRINK.

I DON'T KNOW WHERE HE WENT, THOUGH...
THANK YOU!
SAITO-SAN DOESN'T HAVE A FAVORITE PLACE.
HE LIKES TO GO AROUND TO DIFFERENT PLACES AND DRINK ALONE...
SO THERE'S NO GUARANTEE THAT I WILL BE ABLE TO FIND HIM.
BUT ...
...THAT'S STILL BETTER THAN WAITING AT HEADQUARTERS!
WHAT IS THE MEANING OF THIS...
...SEIZABURO?

YES, SIR.
YOU ARE A MAN OF TASTE, UKINOSUKE-SAMA, SO I THOUGHT IT WOULD BE BORING IF WE WENT RIGHT TO SLEEP.
THAT IS WHY I PREPARED A FEAST, FIRST.
OOOH. ♡
HE IS SO HANDSOME!
THANK YOU VERY MUCH FOR INVITING US.♡
HMM...
THAT'S FINE, BUT...
WE ARE TSURU AND MATSU.
LET'S GET TO KNOW EACH OTHER OVER A DRINK. ♡
I'LL MAKE HIM DRINK AS MUCH AS POSSIBLE, TO START WITH.
IDEALLY, HE WILL PASS OUT DRUNK.
BUT EVEN IF HE GETS SLIGHTLY GROGGY, IT WILL BE A LOT EASIER FOR ME TO DEAL WITH HIM.

I WILL NEVER ALLOW SUCH A TEMPERAMENTAL MAN TO TWIST ME AROUND HIS LITTLE FINGER!
I WON'T LET HIM DECIDE THE BAKUFU'S FATE...
...OVER A STUPID WAGER LIKE THIS!!
SEIZABURO!
YES SIR!
YOU DRINK TOO!
UKI-SAMA.
ISN'T HE A BUSHI?
HE'LL GET ANGRY IF YOU TALK TO HIM LIKE THAT.
DON'T WORRY.
I KNOW HIS WEAKNESS, YOU SEE.

OOOH. ♡
I WONDER WHAT HIS WEAKNESS IS.
DRINK, SEIZABURO!
NO...
I AM NOT FOND OF SAKE...
HA HA HA.
I'M DRUNK AND YOU'RE SOBER.
WHAT'S THE FUN IN THAT, EH?
TCH, HE NOTICED.
HE CAN'T BE UNDERESTIMATED.
I'M SORRY.
TO BE HONEST, I HAVE BEEN TOLD THAT I CANNOT HOLD MY LIQUOR.
I DON'T REMEMBER ANYTHING, BUT APPARENTLY I HAVE PUNCHED AND KICKED MY COMRADES COUNTLESS TIMES...
OH MY, IS THAT TRUE?
BUT YOU LOOK SO CUTE...
INTERESTING.
I WANT TO SEE YOU LIKE THAT!

YOU'RE GOING TO REGRET IT...
THE FOOL FELL FOR IT!
NO MATTER WHAT I DO OR SAY...
...IT WILL NOW BE HIS RESPONSIBILITY FOR MAKING ME DRINK.
YOU HAVE SUCH ALLURING EYES, SEIZABURO. ♡
JUST COME OVER HERE.
WHAT ...
FWIP
I'LL TAKE MY TIME...
AAAH, UKI-SAMA!
UKI...!
CLATTER
...AND TEACH YOU THE RIGHT WAY TO DRINK SAKE.

GULP
...!
GOOD, ISN'T IT...
... SEIZABURO?
HEY, SOJI!
IT'S RARE TO SEE YOU IN A PLACE LIKE THIS.
NAGAKURA-SAN, TODO-SAN!
HAVE YOU SEEN SAITO-SAN?

EEH?
I THINK WE SAW HIM SOME-WHERE.
HE LEFT JUST AS WE ENTERED!
THE BAR IN FRONT OF THE GION SHRINE.
HOW LONG AGO WAS THAT?
AN HOUR?
JOIN US FOR A DRINK, SOJI!
SORRY, I NEED TO SEE SAITO-SAN TONIGHT!
DID HE GO WEST OR SOUTH ...
...FROM THE GION SHRINE...?
A FEW BLOCKS NORTH OF THIS STREET...
...IS THE HOTEL ROOM WHERE KAMIYA-SAN IS...

"I WILL NOT REGRET OFFERING MYSELF FOR THIS MISSION."
IT CANNOT BE EASY FOR HER...
...AS A GIRL, TO CHOOSE TO SLEEP WITH A MAN SHE DOESN'T EVEN LIKE ...
LOOK!
IT'S A BRIDAL PROCES-SION!
OO-OOH.
WHAT A FINE PROCES-SION!
OF COURSE, IT'S THE MARRIAGE OF FUJIYA'S DAUGHTER.
SHE'S STILL 14 YEARS OLD, BUT SHE'S GOING TO MARRY THE FIFTH MASTER OF KASHIWAYA.
HE'S 18 YEARS OLDER THAN HER.
HE'S OLD ENOUGH TO BE HER FATHER!!
BUT KASHIWAYA IS A POWERFUL MERCHANT WHO EVEN HAS A SHOP IN EDO.
OH...?

IT'S A COMMON THING FOR A GIRL TO BE WITH A MAN WHO SHE HAS NO INTEREST IN...
...JUST FOR HER FAMILY...
AND ON TOP OF THAT, IT'S THE SHOGUN.
NO GIRL WOULD REFUSE IF SHE WERE CHOSEN BY HIM ...
Marrying into money, how nice...
AH?!
COULD IT BE THAT KAMIYA-SAN...
...MADE UP HER MIND SO QUICKLY BECAUSE OF THAT?
SO WHY AM I SO PANICKED?
...
FLOP
Thinking too much.
OH.
WHAT ARE YOU DOING, SOJI?
WE KEEP MEETING TODAY. ♡
Are you here to watch the procession too?

WHAT DO YOU THINK, SEIZABURO?
DRINKING SAKE IN THE ARMS OF A MAN ISN'T SO BAD, IS IT?
...
LET ME SHOW YOU AN EVEN BETTER WAY TO DRINK SAKE.
Oooh.
Hmmm..
WE'RE LUCKY TO BE ABLE TO WATCH THIS.

STOP GETTING CARRIED AWAY, YOU LETCH!!
BA
MM
EEEEEEK!
IT'S NOT RIGHT FOR TWO MEN TO BE DOING SOMETHING LIKE THIS!!
HOW MEAN. BUT YOU DO ALL SORTS OF THINGS WITH OKITA, DON'T YOU?
SHUD-DUP!!
DON'T EVEN COMPARE YOURSELF WITH OKITA SENSEI!!!
HMM-MM.
THEN HOW DOES OKITA TREAT YOU?
I'LL TRY TO DO THE SAME, SO TEACH ME.

NEVEE-EEER!!
AAARGH!
KABLAMM
EEEEEEEK!
HA HA HA HA HA HA HA!
YOU WERE RIGHT! YOU ARE NASTY DRUNK!
TSURU AND MATSU, YOU TWO BETTER LEAVE.
Y-YES, THANK YOU.
GOOD-BYE.
FWIP
BRING... MORE... SAKE!!
STAY HERE!!

SNOOORE
SEIZA-BURO ...?
...
WHAT A CUTE SLEEPING FACE.
SCOOT SCOOT
WHERE SHOULD I START?

HA HA HA HA.
YOU TOSS AND TURN IN YOUR SLEEP, TOO!
ROLL ROLL ROLL ROLL
HMMFF...
YOU'LL NEVER SURVIVE UNTIL THE MORNING...
...IF YOU'RE ALREADY PRETENDING TO BE DRUNK, SEIZABURO.
TCH!
SO YOU NOTICED.
TUPP
HA HA HA HA HA.
YOU REALLY ARE A FUNNY GUY.
I LIKE YOU EVEN MORE!
WHAT?
RUSTLE

!!
I SHALL NOT ALLOW ANY RESISTANCE FROM NOW ON, SEIZABURO!
DID YOU NOT...
...AGREE TO SLEEP WITH THE 15TH SHOGUN, TOKUGAWA YOSHINOBU, TONIGHT?!
A-AS YOU WISH!
I CAN'T REJECT HIM...
...IF HE ORDERS ME IN THE NAME OF THE SHOGUN.
DON'T WORRY.
I'LL BE KIND TO YOU.
I HAVE NO OTHER CHOICE.
THIS GUY IS INTERESTED IN ME, EVEN THOUGH HE HAS TEN BEAUTIFUL CONCUBINES...
...BECAUSE HE THINKS I AM A MAN.

TO BE CONTINUED!

TAEKO WATANABE PRESENTS

*Sorry to keep you waiting.

NOW THEN, LAST TIME I TALKED MAINLY ABOUT CANDLES ...
...BUT CANDLES WERE ACTUALLY QUITE A LUXURY ITEM BACK THEN.
LANTERNS ARE USEFUL, BUT EXPENSIVE...
...SO THEY WERE MOSTLY USED BY BUSHI FAMILIES AND RED LIGHT DISTRICT WORKERS.
COMMONERS DIDN'T GO OUT AFTER DARK.
誠
SO THE MAIN FORM OF ILLU-MINATION USED BY THE COMMON PEOPLE WAS OIL LAMPS.
SEVERAL HUNDRED YEARS OLDER THAN CANDLES!!
WICK
OIL
WICK HOLDER
OIL LAMP STAND + PLATE
A FLAME WAS LIT ON WICKS THAT WERE USUALLY DIPPED IN RAPESEED OR SESAME SEED OIL...
...BUT OIL FROM SARDINES AND OTHER FISH WAS CHEAPER, AND WAS SAID TO HAVE A VERY FOUL SMELL.
PUT OUT A LOT OF SMOKE TOO
IT STINKS !!
OH. THIS BRINGS BACK MEMO-RIES.
FROM A VERY POOR FAMILY
ALSO, THE WICK NEEDED TO BE PULLED OUT QUITE FRE-QUENTLY ...
...OR ELSE THE FIRE WOULD EXTIN-GUISH!

HOWEVER, THE INVENTION OF OIL LAMPS MADE THE EXTREMELY DANGEROUS ACT OF LIGHTING FIRE IN A ROOM MUCH SAFER...
...AND YOU COULD ADJUST THEIR BRIGHTNESS BY ADDING OR REMOVING WICKS. SO IN SOME WAYS I THINK YOU CAN CLAIM THAT THE INFLUENCE OF OIL LAMPS ON HUMAN LIFE WAS AS GREAT AS THE JUMP FROM CANDLES TO LIGHT BULBS.
WHAT KIND OF LIGHTS DID PEOPLE USE INSIDE THEIR HOUSES BEFORE THAT?
THEY'D BURN PINE ROOTS, LIKE THIS.
STATIONARY TYPES WITH PINE ROOTS THAT ARE BROKEN APART AND BURNT.
PINE LAMP, IRON
PINE ROOT BRAZIER, STONE
PORTABLE TYPES, SUCH AS THIN STICKS THAT WERE LIT AT THE TIP.
THESE WERE OIL TORCHES ...
THEY WERE BURNT AT THE TIP WITH CHARCOAL, AND COATED WITH OIL TO PROVIDE FOR EASY LIGHTING.
ABOUT 18 INCHES
PAPER WRAPPED AROUND THE HANDLE
...BUT LATER EVOLVED INTO PAPER TORCHES, WHICH WERE WRAPPED PAPER COATED WITH CANDLE WAX OR OIL.
PEOPLE WOULD USE THE PAPER TORCH WHEN GOING OUT TO USE THE TOILET AND WHATNOT.
Why are we in the bedroom?
IT WAS USED TO GET RID OF MOSQUITOS INSIDE A MOSQUITO NET TOO!
BZZZZZZ
SZZL
AND NOW ...
...LET ME INTRODUCE YOU TO VARIOUS OIL LAMP APPARATUS!
LET'S GO!!

FIRST, THE VERY BASIC ...
... SQUARE LANTERN.
OIL CAN
☆ OFTEN USED IN THE KANTO REGION
AND THE CYLINDRICAL ENSHU LANTERN.
☆ OFTEN USED IN THE KANSAI REGION
ONE SIDE OF THE LANTERN WOULD OPEN UP...
...WHICH MADE IT EASY TO ADD THE OIL AS WELL AS ADJUST ITS BRIGHTNESS.
THE ARIAKE LANTERN WAS EVEN MORE EXCEPTIONAL ...
☆ THIS IS HOW IT WAS USUALLY USED.
BUT YOU COULD SWITCH THE TOP AND BOTTOM...
☆ SLEEPING ROOM CONFIGURATION ①
②
③
...AND IT COULD BE USED IN VARIOUS CONFIGURATIONS!

Kaze Hikaru Diary R: The End

Decoding Kaze Hikaru

Kaze Hikaru is a historical drama based in 19th century Japan and thus contains some fairly mystifying terminology. In this glossary we'll break down archaic phrases, terms and other linguistic curiosities for you so that you can move through life with the smug assurance that you are indeed a know-it-all.

First and foremost, because *Kaze Hikaru* is a period story, we kept all character names in their traditional Japanese form—that is, family name followed by first name. For example, the character Okita Soji's family name is Okita and his personal name is Soji.

BAKUFU:
Literally, "tent government." Shogunate; the feudal, military government that dominated Japan for more than 200 years.

BUSHI:
A samurai or warrior (part of the compound word *bushido*, which means "way of the warrior").

CASTELLA/KASUTERA:
A traditional Japanese sponge cake of Portuguese origin.

-CHAN:
A diminutive suffix that conveys endearment.

DAIMYO:
A landholding feudal lord.

EDO:
The former name of Tokyo.

GION:
Kyoto's entertainment district.

GOCHO:
The rank below assistant vice captain in the Shinsengumi hierarchy.

HAN:
A feudal domain of Japan during the Edo period.

HOGEN:
The second-highest rank among private doctors within the bakufu, the highest being *Hoin*.

IKEDAYA INCIDENT:
A Shinsengumi raid on an inn in Kyoto where anti-Shogunate rebels had gathered. Seven rebels were killed and scores were arrested.

JIZO STATUE:
A serenely smiling Buddhist statue.

-KO:
An honorific suffix added to the names of lords and those of high status.

KOSHO:
A Shinsengumi captain's personal assistant.

-KUN:
An honorific suffix that indicates a difference in rank and title. The use of *-kun* is also a way of indicating familiarity and friendliness between students or compatriots.

MACE:
A term derived from the Dutch word *Meester*, meaning Master.

ONI:
Literally, "ogre."

RONIN:
Masterless samurai.

-SAMA:
An honorific suffix used for one of higher rank; a more respectful version of *-san*.

-SAN:
An honorific suffix that carries the meaning of "Mr." or "Ms."

SENRYU:
A humorous, haiku-like poem.

SENSEI:
A teacher, master or instructor.

SHIMABARA:
Formerly the red-light district in Kyoto.

SHUDO:
A romantic relationship between a younger samurai and his older mentor.

TEN'NEN RISHIN-RYU:
The form of martial art practiced by members of the Shinsengumi.

In the last volume I carelessly wrote about the promotional copy that appeared on the comic book's obi strip and then realized, "Shoot! People who bought the second printing will have no idea what I'm talking about!!" But it was too late (sweat).* Sorry. I decided to never talk about this again...but let me talk about it one last time: I want to brag on and on about how honored I was to have Takashi Yanase Sensei draw an illustration of Anpanman in a Shinsengumi uniform (*haha*). Thank you very much, Sensei!!** Anyway, the seasonal term for this volume is "steamy breath." Troop duty during winter must be tough, but doesn't it warm your heart to think that when Soji's looking spaced out, he's actually thinking, "How can I warm up Kamiya-san's hands...?" (*haha*).

*The promotional copy and obi strip that Watanabe Sensei mentions here were not included with the English version of Volume 27.

**Takashi Yanase is a famous Japanese writer, poet and illustrator. He's renowned for his Anpanman character, a children's picture book and anime hero with the face of a red bean bun.

Taeko Watanabe debuted as a manga artist in 1979 with her story *Waka-chan no Netsuai Jidai* (Love Struck Days of Waka). *Kaze Hikaru* is her longest-running series, but she has created a number of other popular series. Watanabe is a two-time winner of the prestigious Shogakukan Manga Award in the girls' category—her manga *Hajime-chan ga Ichiban!* (Hajime-chan Is Number One!) claimed the award in 1991, and *Kaze Hikaru* took it in 2003.

Watanabe read hundreds of historical sources to create *Kaze Hikaru*. She is from Tokyo.

KAZE HIKARU
VOL. 28
Shojo Beat Edition

STORY AND ART BY
TAEKO WATANABE

Translation & English Adaptation/Tetsuichiro Miyaki
Touch-up Art & Lettering/Rina Mapa
Design/J. Shikuma
Editor/Megan Bates

Printed in the U.S.A.

Published by VIZ Media, LLC
P.O. Box 77010
San Francisco, CA 94107

10 9 8 7 6 5 4 3 2 1
First printing, August 2020

viz.com

PARENTAL ADVISORY
KAZE HIKARU is rated T+ for Older Teen and is recommended for ages 16 and up. This volume contains realistic violence, alcohol use and sexual themes.

RATED T+ OLDER TEEN ratings.viz.com

shojobeat.com

SURPRISE!

You may be reading the wrong way!

It's true: In keeping with the original Japanese comic format, this book reads from right to left—so action, sound effects, and word balloons are completely reversed. This preserves the orientation of the original artwork—plus, it's fun! Check out the diagram shown here to get the hang of things, and then turn to the other side of the book to get started!

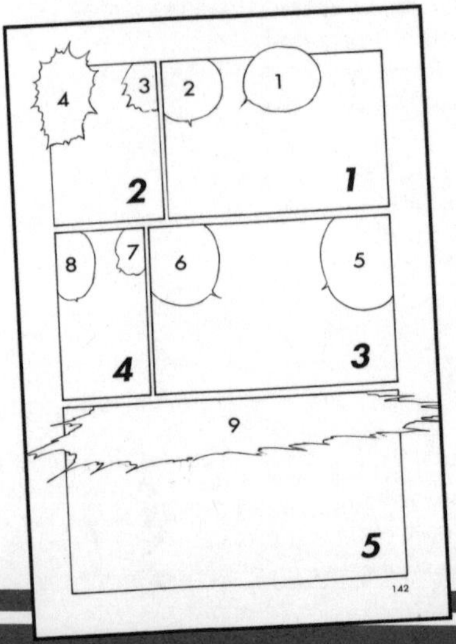